Voices of Our Kind

Third Edition

An Anthology of Modern Scottish Poetry from 1920 to the Present

Edited by
Alexander Scott

'. . . and it wasn't the words or tune. It was the singing.
It was the human sweetness in that yellow,
the unpredicted voices of our kind.'

Iain Crichton Smith

Published in association with The Saltire Society
and the Scots Language Society

Chambers

© Introduction and selection
  Alexander Scott 1987

First published by The Saltire Society 1971
Second edition 1975
Third edition published by W & R Chambers Ltd, Edinburgh 1987

The publisher acknowledges subsidy from the Scottish Arts Council towards the
publication of this volume.

British Library Cataloguing in Publication Data
Scott, Alexander
  Voices of our kind: an anthology of modern Scottish poetry from 1920 to the
  present.
  —3rd ed.
  1. Scottish poetry   2. English poetry
  —Scottish authors
  I. Title
  821'.912'08   PR8658

  ISBN 0–550–20495–4

Jacket design by James Hutcheson
Typeset by Buccleuch Printers Ltd, Hawick.
Printed by Martin's of Berwick.

Voices of Our Kind

Also published by Chambers
Scottish Nursery Rhymes

Voices of Our Kind

Alexander Scott retired as Head of the Department of Scottish Literature at the University of Glasgow in 1983. He was the founding editor of the annual *New Writing Scotland* and is well known as a poet, biographer and dramatist.

Acknowledgements

The editor gratefully acknowledges permission from the following: Mrs Paddy Fraser, for the poems by G. S. Fraser; Mrs Helen Willis and Mr Ian G. Sutherland, for the poems by Robert Garioch; Mrs Nessie Graham, for the poems by W. S. Graham; the Trustees of the W. L. Lorimer Memorial Trust and the holder of the Copyright for the poems by George Campbell Hay; Mr Michael Grieve, for the poems by Hugh MacDiarmid; Mrs Isabella Mackie, for the poems by A. D. Mackie; Mrs Kathleen McLellan, for the poem by Robert McLellan; Mrs Hazel Smith, for the poems by Sydney Goodsir Smith; the Trustees of the National Library of Scotland, for the poems by William Soutar; Mrs Hella Young, for the poems by Douglas Young; and, for their own poems, James Aitchison, J. K. Annand, Alan Bold, George Mackay Brown, George Bruce, Tom Buchan, Donald Campbell, Stewart Conn, Robert Crawford, Valerie Gillies, Duncan Glen, Stanley Roger Green, Andrew Greig, T. S. Law, Tom Leonard, Maurice Lindsay, Liz Lochhead, Donald Macaulay, Norman MacCaig, Sorley Maclean, William Montgomerie, Edwin Morgan, Ken Morrice, Stephen Mulrine, Tom Scott, Iain Crichton Smith, William J. Tait, Derick Thomson, Raymond Vettese, Roderick Watson.

Acknowledgement is also made to the following publishers: Aberdeen University Press for the poem by Charles Murray and the poems by Alastair Mackie and Christopher Rush; Faber and Faber for the poems by Edwin Muir and Douglas Dunn.

Published in association with The Saltire Society and the Scots Language Society.

The Saltire Society was founded in 1936 to work for the revival of the distinctive cultural life of Scotland. Since then it has been active in the preservation of all that is best in Scottish tradition and in the encouragement of new developments likely to strengthen and enrich the cultural life of the country. Membership is open to all who share these objectives. Details from the Society at 13 Atholl Crescent, Edinburgh EH3 8HA. Telephone 031–228 6621.

The Scots Language Society was founded in 1972 to promote Scots in literature, drama, the media, education and in everyday usage. Since Scots was once the state language, it is a valid part of Scotland's heritage. The Society believes it should now take its rightful place as a language of Scotland along with Gaelic and English.

Contents

Introduction

This most widely-read of modern Scottish poetry anthologies, first appearing in 1971, was originally designed for use in schools and was prepared for publication by Dr Maurice Lindsay on behalf of the Glasgow Schools Scottish Literary Committee. So successful was the selection that a second edition followed in 1975, revised by a practising schoolteacher, Miss Morven Cameron, in the light of experience of teaching Scottish poetry to Glasgow children.

However, the anthology has found favour with university students and with general readers too, and consequently this new edition has been prepared with that wider readership also in mind. This time the book's range has been greatly increased by matching the representation of poetry in English with that of poetry in Scots, while work in Gaelic, which had previously appeared only in translation, is now published in the original language as well as in English versions.

In the sixteen years since the first edition, many new poets have emerged, and they are represented here alongside the recent work of established writers, thereby presenting a picture of modern Scottish poetry unmatched by any other selection. The richness of the writing produced, in all three of the languages used in Scotland, has made the editorial work highly rewarding, and it is hoped that the resulting selection (and re-selection) will give pleasure to a new generation of readers, both in and out of school.

The year 1920, in which this book begins, saw the publication of the last volume of verse written by Charles Murray, the outstanding Scots poet of the first two decades of this century, and of the first anthology edited by C. M. Grieve, who was shortly to adopt the pseudonym of Hugh MacDiarmid and emerge as our greatest poet since Burns. In Murray's last poems, as in MacDiarmid's first, Scots verse ceased to be insular and became universal in its implications without loss of nationality of tone. Scottish poets writing in English and Gaelic were also stimulated to similar endeavour, and the movement thus inaugurated has continued to this day.

Alexander Scott,
Research Fellow in Scottish Literature,
University of Glasgow

CHARLES MURRAY

GIN I WAS GOD

Gin I was God, sittin' up there abeen,
Weariet nae doot noo a' my darg was deen,
Deaved wi' the harps an' hymns oonendin' ringin',
Tired o' the flockin' angels hairse wi' singin',
To some clood-edge I'd daunder furth an', feth,
Look ower an' watch hoo things were gyaun aneth.
Syne, gin I saw hoo men I'd made mysel'
Had startit in to pooshan, sheet an' fell,
To reive an' rape, an' fairly mak' a hell
O' my braw birlin' Earth, – a hale week's wark –
I'd cast my coat again, rowe up my sark,
An', or they'd time to lench a second ark,
Tak' back my word an' sen' anither spate,
Droon oot the hale hypothec, dicht the sklate,
Own my mistak', an', aince I'd cleared the brod,
Start a'thing ower again, gin I was God.

abeen, above; *weariet*, exhausted; *darg*, work; *deen*, done; *deaved*, deafened;
daunder furth, stroll forth; *feth*, truly; *gyaun aneth*, going below; *pooshan*, poison;
sheet, shoot; *reive*, plunder; *braw*, fine; *birlin'*, whirling; *hale*, whole; *rowe*, roll; *sark*,
shirt; *lench*, launch; *hypothec*, concern; *dicht*, wipe; *sklate*, slate; *brod*, board;
a'thing, everything

EDWIN MUIR

SCOTLAND'S WINTER

Now the ice lays its smooth claws on the sill,
The sun looks from the hill
Helmed in his winter casket,
And sweeps his arctic sword across the sky.

The water at the mill
Sounds more hoarse and dull.
The miller's daughter walking by
With frozen fingers soldered to her basket
Seems to be knocking
Upon a hundred leagues of floor
With her light heels, and mocking
Percy and Douglas dead,
And Bruce on his burial bed,
Where he lies white as may
With wars and leprosy,
And all the kings before
This land was kingless,
And all the singers before
This land was songless,
This land that with its dead and living
    waits the Judgement Day.
But they, the powerless dead,
Listening can hear no more
Than a hard tapping on the floor
A little overhead
Of common heels that do not know
Whence they come or where they go
And are content
With their poor frozen life and shallow banishment.

A BIRTHDAY

I never felt so much
Since I have felt at all
The tingling smell and touch
Of dogrose and sweet briar,
Nettles against the wall,

All sours and sweets that grow
Together or apart
In hedge or marsh or ditch.
I gather to my heart
Beast, insect, flower, earth, water, fire,
In absolute desire,
As fifty years ago.

Acceptance, gratitude:
The first look and the last
When all between has passed
Restore ingenuous good
That seeks no personal end,
Nor strives to mar or mend.
Before I touched the food
Sweetness ensnared my tongue;
Before I saw the wood
I loved each nook and bend,
The track going right and wrong;
Before I took the road
Direction ravished my soul.
Now that I can discern
It whole or almost whole,
Acceptance and gratitude
Like travellers return
And stand where they first stood.

THE HORSES

Barely a twelvemonth after
The seven days war that put the world to sleep,
Late in the evening the strange horses came.
By then we had made our covenant with silence,

But in the first few days it was so still
We listened to our breathing and were afraid.
On the second day
The radios failed; we turned the knobs; no answer.
On the third day a warship passed us, heading north,
Dead bodies piled on the deck. On the sixth day
A plane plunged over us into the sea. Thereafter
Nothing. The radios dumb;
And still they stand in corners of our kitchens,
And stand, perhaps, turned on, in a million rooms
All over the world. But now if they should speak,
If on a sudden they should speak again,
If on the stroke of noon a voice should speak,
We would not listen, we would not let it bring
That old bad world that swallowed its children quick
At one great gulp. We would not have it again.
Sometimes we think of the nations lying asleep,
Curled blindly in impenetrable sorrow,
And then the thought confounds us with its strangeness.
The tractors lie about our fields; at evening
They look like dank sea-monsters couched and waiting.
We leave them where they are and let them rust:
'They'll moulder away and be like other loam.'
We make our oxen drag our rusty ploughs,
Long laid aside. We have gone back
Far past our fathers' land.

                           And then, that evening
Late in the summer the strange horses came.
We heard a distant tapping on the road,
A deepening drumming; it stopped, went on again
And at the corner changed to hollow thunder.
We saw the heads
Like a wild wave charging and were afraid.

We had sold our horses in our fathers' time
To buy new tractors. Now they were strange to us
As fabulous steeds set on an ancient shield
Or illustrations in a book of knights.
We did not dare go near them. Yet they waited,
Stubborn and shy, as if they had been sent
By an old command to find our whereabouts
And that long-lost archaic companionship.
In the first moment we had never a thought
That they were creatures to be owned and used.
Among them were some half-a-dozen colts
Dropped in some wilderness of the broken world,
Yet new as if they had come from their own Eden.
Since then they have pulled our ploughs and borne our loads,
But that free servitude still can pierce our hearts.
Our life is changed; their coming our beginning.

HUGH MACDIARMID

THE BONNIE BROUKIT BAIRN

Mars is braw in crammasy,
Venus in a green silk goun,
The auld mune shak's her gowden feathers,
Their starry talk's a wheen o' blethers,
Nane for thee a thochtie sparin',
Earth, thou bonnie broukit bairn!
— *But greet, an' in your tears ye'll droun
The haill clanjamfrie!*

bonnie, beautiful; *broukit*, grimy, tear-stained; *braw*, handsome; *crammasy*,
crimson; *wheen o' blethers*, quantity of nonsense; *greet*, weep; *clanjamfrie*,
collection

O JESU PARVULE

'Followis ane sang of the birth of Christ, with the tune of Baw lu la law.'
—Godly Ballates

His mither sings to the bairnie Christ
Wi' the tune o' *Baw lu la law.*
The bonnie wee craturie lauchs in His crib
An' a' the starnies an' he are sib.
    Baw, baw, my loonikie, baw, balloo.

'Fa' owre, ma hinny, fa' owre, fa' owre,
A' body's sleepin' binna oorsels.'
She's drawn Him in tae the bool o' her breist
But the byspale's nae thocht o' sleep i' the least.
    Balloo, wee mannie, balloo, balloo.

sib, akin, friendly; *loonikie*, wee boy; *binna*, except; *byspale*, a child of whom wonderful things are expected

THE INNUMERABLE CHRIST

'Other stars may have their Bethlehem, and their Calvary too.'
Professor J. Y. Simpson

Wha kens on whatna Bethlehems
Earth twinkles like a star the nicht,
An' whatna shepherds lift their heids
    In its unearthly licht?

'Yont a' the stars oor een can see
An' farther than their lichts can fly,
I' mony an unco warl' the nicht
    The fatefu' bairnies cry.

I' mony an unco warl' the nicht
The lift gaes black as pitch at noon,
An' sideways on their chests the heids
   O' endless Christs roll doon.

An' when the earth's as cauld's the mune
An' a' its folk are lang syne deid,
On coontless stars the Babe maun cry
   An' the Crucified maun bleed.

unco, strange; *lift*, sky

CROWDIEKNOWE

Oh to be at Crowdieknowe
When the last trumpet blaws,
An' see the deid come loupin' owre
The auld grey wa's.

Muckle men wi' tousled beards,
I grat at as a bairn
'll scramble frae the croodit clay
Wi' feck o' swearin'

An' glower at God an' a' his gang
O' angels i' the lift
— Thae trashy bleezin' French-like folk
Wha gar'd them shift!

Fain the weemun-folk'll seek
To mak' them haud their row
— *Fegs, God's no blate gin he stirs up*
The men o' Crowdieknowe!

Crowdieknowe, graveyard near Langholm; *loupin' owre*, leaping over; *muckle*,
huge; *grat*, wept; *feck*, abundance; *lift*, sky; *gar'd*, caused to; *blate*, timid

EMPTY VESSEL

I met ayont the cairney
A lass wi' tousie hair
Singin' till a bairnie
That was nae langer there.

Wunds wi warlds to swing
Dinna sing sae sweet,
The licht that bends owre a'thing
Is less ta'en up wi't.

wunds, winds; *a'thing*, everything; *ta'en up wi't*, preoccupied with it

THE EEMIS STANE

I' the how-dumb-deid o' the cauld hairst nicht
The warl' like an eemis stane
Wags i' the lift;
An' my eerie memories fa'
Like a yowdendrift.

Like a yowdendrift so's I couldna read
The words cut oot i' the stane
Had the fug o' fame
An' history's hazelraw
No' yirdit thaim.

eemis, unsteady; *how-dumb-deid*, dead silent depth; *cauld hairst nicht*, cold harvest
night; *lift*, sky; *yowdendrift*, blizzard; *fug*, moss; *hazelraw*, lichen; *yirdit*, buried

FOCHERTY

Duncan Gibb o' Focherty's
A giant to the likes o' me,
His face is like a roarin' fire
For love o' the barley-bree.

He gangs through this and the neebrin' shire
Like a muckle rootless tree
— And here's a caber for Daith to toss
That'll gi'e his spauld a swee!

His gain was aye a wee'r man's loss
And he took my lass frae me,
An wi' mony a quean besides
He's ta'en his liberty.

I've had nae chance wi' the likes o' him
And he's tramped me underfit.
— Blaefaced afore the throne o' God
He'll get his fairin' yet.

He'll be like a bull in the sale-ring there,
And I'll lauch lood to see,
Till he looks up and canna mak' oot
Whether it's God — or me!

barley-bree, whisky; *gangs*, goes; *neebrin'*, neighbouring; *spauld*, backbone; *swee*,
jerk; *wee'r*, lesser; *quean*, lass; *blaefaced*, livid with fear; *fairin'*, deserts

SIC TRANSIT GLORIA SCOTIAE

I amna fou' sae muckle as tired – deid dune.
It's gey and hard wark coupin' gless for gless
Wi' Cruivie and Gilsanquhar and the like,
And I'm no' juist as bauld as aince I wes.

The elbuck fankles in the coorse o' time,
The sheckle's no' sae souple, and the thrapple
Grows deef and dour: nae langer up and doun
Gleg as a squirrel speils the Adam's apple.

Forbye, the stuffie's no' the real Mackay.
. The sun's sel' aince, as sune as ye began it,
Riz in your vera saul: but what keeks in
Noo is in truth the vilest 'saxpenny planet.'

And as the worth's gane doun the cost has risen.
Yin canna thow the cockles o' yin's hert
Wi'oot ha'en' cauld feet noo, jalousin' what
The wife'll say (I dinna blame her fur't).

It's robbin' Peter to pey Paul at least. . . .
And a' that's Scotch aboot it is the name,
Like a'thing else ca'd Scottish nooadays
– A' destitute o' speerit juist the same.

(To prove my saul is Scots I maun begin
Wi' what's still deemed Scots and the folk expect,
And spire up syne by visible degrees
To heichts whereo' the fules ha'e never recked.

But aince I get them there I'll whummle them
And souse the craturs in the nether deeps,
— For it's nae choice, and ony man s'ud wish
To dree the goat's weird tae as weel's the sheep's!)

Heifetz in tartan, and Sir Harry Lauder!
Whaur's Isadora Duncan dancin' noo?
Is Mary Garden in Chicago still
And Duncan Grant in Paris — and me fou'?

Sic transit gloria Scotiae — a' the floo'ers
O' the Forest are wede awa'. (A blin' bird's nest
Is aiblins biggin' in the thistle tho'? . . .
And better blin' if'ts brood is like the rest!)

You canna gang to a Burns supper even
Wi'oot some wizened scrunt o' a knock-knee
Chinee turns roon to say, 'Him Haggis — velly goot!'
And ten to wan the piper is a Cockney.

No' wan in fifty kens a wurd Burns wrote
But misapplied is a'body's property,
And gin there was his like alive the day
They'd be the last a kennin' haund to gi'e —

Croose London Scotties wi' their braw shirt fronts
And a' their fancy freen's, rejoicin'
That similah gatherings in Timbuctoo,
Bagdad — and Hell, nae doot — are voicin'

Burns' sentiments o' universal love,
In pidgin English or in wild-fowl Scots,
And toastin' ane wha's nocht to them but an
Excuse for faitherin' Genius wi *their* thochts.

A' *they*'ve to say was aften said afore
A lad was born in Kyle to blaw aboot.
What unco fate mak's *him* the dumpin'-grun'
For a' the sloppy rubbish they jaw oot?

Mair nonsense has been uttered in his name
Than in ony's barrin' liberty and Christ.
If this keeps spreedin' as the drink declines,
Syne turns to tea, wae's me for the *Zeitgeist*!

Rabbie, wad'st thou wert here – the warld hath need,
And Scotland mair sae, o' the likes o' thee!
The whisky that aince moved your lyre's become
A laxative for a' loquacity.

O gin they'd stegh their guts and haud their wheesht
I'd thole it, for 'a man's a man' I ken,
But though the feck ha'e plenty o' the 'a' that',
They're nocht but zoologically men.

I'm haverin', Rabbie, but ye understaun'
It gets my dander up to see your star
A bauble in Babel, banged like a saxpence
'Twixt Burbank's Baedeker and Bleistein's cigar.

There's nane sae ignorant but think they can
Expatiate on *you*, if on nae ither.
The sumphs ha'e ta'en you at your wurd, and, fegs!
The foziest o' them claims to be a – Brither!

Syne 'Here's the cheenge' – the star o' Rabbie Burns.
Sma' cheenge, 'Twinkle, Twinkle.' The memory slips
As G. K. Chesterton heaves up to gi'e
'The Immortal Memory' in a huge eclipse,

Or somebody else as famous if less fat.
You left the like in Embro in a scunner
To booze wi' thieveless cronies sic as me.
I'se warrant you'd shy clear o' a' the hunner

Odd Burns Clubs tae, or ninety-nine o' them,
And haud your birthday in a different kip
Whaur your name isna ta'en in vain — as Christ
Gied a' Jerusalem's Pharisees the slip

— Christ wha'd ha'e been Chief Rabbi gin he'd lik't!
Wi' publicans and sinners to forgether,
But, losh! the publicans noo are Pharisees,
And I'm no' shair o' maist the sinners either.

But that's aside the point! I've got fair waun'ert.
It's no' that I'm sae fou' as just deid dune,
And dinna ken as muckle's whaur I am
Or hoo I've come to sprawl here 'neth the mune.

That's it! It isna me that's fou' at a',
But the fu' mune, the doited jade, that's led
Me fer agley, or 'mogrified the warld.
— For a' I ken I'm safe in my ain bed.

Jean! Jean! Gin *she's* no' here it's no' *oor* bed,
Or else I'm dreamin' deep and canna wauken,
But it's a feel queer dream if this is no'
A real hillside — and thae things thistles and bracken!

It's hard wark haud'n by a thocht worth ha'en'
And harder speakin't, and no' for ilka man;
Maist Thocht's like whisky — a thoosan' under proof,
And a sair price is pitten on't even than.

As Kirks wi' Christianity ha'e dune,
Burns Clubs wi' Burns — wi' a'thing it's the same,
The core o' ocht is only for the few,
Scorned by the mony, thrang wi'ts empty name.

And a' the names in History mean nocht
To maist folk but 'ideas o' their ain,'
The vera opposite o' onything
The Deid 'ud awn gin they cam' back again.

A greater Christ, a greater Burns, may come.
The maist they'll dae is to gi'e bigger pegs
To folly and conceit to hank their rubbish on.
They'll cheenge folks' talk but no' their natures, fegs!

fou', drunk; *muckle*, much; *deid dune*, completely exhausted; *coupin'*, emptying; *bauld*, bold; *elbuck*, elbow; *fankles*, becomes clumsy; *sheckle*, wrist; *thrapple*, windpipe; *dour*, stubborn; *gleg*, nimble; *speils*, climbs; *sun's sel'*, sun itself; *aince*, once; *riz*, rose; *keeks*, peeps; *thow*, thaw; *jalousin'*, guessing; *speerit*, spirit; *maun*, must; *spire*, soar; *syne*, then; *whummle*, overturn; *dree*, suffer, endure; *weird*, fate; *tae*, also; *wede awa'*, withered; *aiblins*, perhaps; *biggin'*, building; *scrunt*, dwarf; *gin*, if; *kennin'*, understanding; *croose*, self-satisfied; *unco*, extraordinary; *stegh*, stuff; *haud their wheesht*, keep quiet; *thole*, endure; *feck*, majority; *dander*, temper; *sumphs*, fools; *fegs*, truly; *foziest*, softest; *scunner*, disgust; *thieveless*, worthless; *I'se*, I should; *kip*, place; *shair*, sure; *waun'ert*, led astray; *'neth*, beneath; *doited*, crazed; *agley*, astray; *'mogrified*, transformed; *haud'n*, holding; *ilka*, every; *pitten*, put; *ocht*, anything; *thrang*, busy; *'ud awn*, would own; *hank*, fasten

LOURD ON MY HERT

Lourd on my hert as winter lies
The state that Scotland's in the day.
Spring to the North has aye come slow
But now dour winter's like to stay
    For guid,
        And no' for guid!

O wae's me on the weary days
When it is scarce grey licht at noon;
It maun be a' the stupid folk
Diffusin' their dullness roon and roon
    Like soot
    That keeps the sunlicht oot.

Nae wonder if I think I see
A lichter shadow than the neist
I'm fain to cry: 'The dawn, the dawn!
I see it brakin' in the East.'
    But ah
    — It's juist mair snaw!

lourd, heavy; *dour*, hard, grim; *guid*, good; *wae's me on*, alas for; *neist*, next

AT MY FATHER'S GRAVE

The sunlicht still on me, you row'd in clood,
We look upon each ither noo like hills
Across a valley. I'm nae mair your son.
It is my mind, nae son o' yours, that looks,
And the great darkness o' your death comes up
And equals it across the way.
A livin' man upon a deid man thinks
And ony sma'er thocht's impossible.

row'd, wrapped; *sma'er*, smaller

MILK-WORT AND BOG-COTTON

Cwa' een like milk-wort and bog-cotton hair!
I love you, earth, in this mood best o' a'
When the shy spirit like a laich wind moves
And frae the lift nae shadow can fa'
Since there's nocht left to thraw a shadow there
Owre een like milk-wort and milk-white cotton hair.

Wad that nae leaf upon anither wheeled
A shadow either and nae root need dern
In sacrifice to let sic beauty be!
But deep surroondin' darkness I discern
Is aye the price o' licht. Wad licht revealed
Naething but you, and nicht nocht else concealed.

Cwa', come away; *laich*, low; *dern*, hide

WILLIAM SOUTAR

THE CHILDREN

Upon the street they lie
Beside the broken stone:
The blood of children stares from the broken stone.

Death came out of the sky
In the bright afternoon:
Darkness slanted over the bright afternoon.

Again the sky is clear
But upon earth a stain:
The earth is darkened with a darkening stain:

A wound which everywhere
Corrupts the hearts of men:
The blood of children corrupts the hearts of men.

Silence is in the air:
The stars moves to their places:
Silent and serene the stars move to their places:

But from earth the children stare
With blind and fearful faces:
And our charity is in the children's faces.

THE TRYST

O luely, luely, cam she in
And luely she lay doun:
I kent her by her caller lips
And her breists sae sma' and roun'.

A' thru the nicht we spak nae word
Nor sinder'd bane frae bane:
A' thru the nicht I heard her hert
Gang soundin' wi' my ain.

It was about the waukrife hour
Whaun cocks begin to craw
That she smool'd saftly thru the mirk
Afore the day wud daw.

Sae luely, luely, cam she in
Sae luely was she gaen
And wi' her a' my simmer days
Like they had never been.

luely, quietly, softly; *sinder*, to part, sunder; *waukrife*, wakeful; *smool*, to slip away;
mirk, darkness; *daw*, dawn

SONG

Whaur yon broken brig hings owre;
Whaur yon water maks nae soun';
Babylon blaws by in stour:
Gang doun wi' a sang, gang doun.

Deep, owre deep, for onie drouth:
Wan eneuch an ye wud droun:
Saut, or seelfu', for the mouth;
Gang doun wi' a sang, gang doun.

Babylon blaws by in stour
Whaur yon water maks nae soun':
Darkness is your only door;
Gang doun wi' a sang, gang doun.

stour, dust; *saut*, salt; *seelfu'*, pleasant

THE GOWK

Half doun the hill where fa's the linn,
    Far frae the flaught of fowk,
I saw upon a lanely whin,
    A lanely singin' gowk!
       Cuckoo, cuckoo;
And at my my back
The howie hill stude up and spak,
       Cuckoo, cuckoo

There was nae soun': the loupin' linn
Hung frostit in its fa';
Nae bird was on the lanely whin
Sae white wi' fleurs o' snaw:
Cuckoo, cuckoo;
I stude stane still
And saftly spak the howie hill:
Cuckoo, cuckoo.

linn, waterfall; *flaught*, rush; *howie*, hollow

AE NICHT AT AMULREE

Whan Little Dunnin' was a spree,
And no a name as noo,
Wull Todd wha wrocht at Amulree
Gaed hame byordinar fou.

The hairst had a' been gether'd in:
The nicht was snell but clear:
And owre the cantle o' the müne
God keekit here and there.

Whan God saw Wull he gien a lauch
And drappit lichtly doun;
Syne stüde ahint a frostit sauch
Or Wull cam styterin on.

Straucht oot He breeng'd, and blared: 'Wull Todd!'
Blythe as Saint Johnstoun's bell:
'My God!' gowp'd Wull: 'Ye'r richt,' says God:
'I'm gled to meet yersel.'

Little Dunning, annual fair in Perth; *spree*, jollification; *wrocht*, worked;
byordinar fou, extraordinarily drunk; *hairst*, harvest; *snell*, sharp; *cantle*, edge;
keekit, peeped; *gien*, gave; *sauch*, willow; *styterin*, staggering; *breeng'd*, moved
impetuously; *Saint Johnstoun*, Perth

COMPENSATION

Stumpy Dunn, like a fell lot mair
Wha straid awa sae trig,
Has traikit hame again frae the war
Wi' a medal and a lang pin-leg.

Up wi' your gless for Stumpy Dunn
And lat there be nae stint;
We're nae owre shair o' what he has won
But we're shair o' what he has tint.

Monie a swankie, wha aince was here
And swackit aff his swig,
Wud think it weel to be hame frae the war
Wi' a medal and a lang pin-leg.

stumpy, amputated leg; *fell*, exceeding; *straid*, strode; *trig*, smart; *traikit*, walked
with difficulty; *pin-leg*, wooden leg; *tint*, lost; *swankie*, active youngster; *swackit*,
drank deeply

THE PHILOSOPHIC TAED

There was a taed wha thocht sae lang
On sanctity and sin;
On what was richt, and what was wrang,
And what was in atween –
That he gat naething düne.

The wind micht blaw, the snaw micht snaw,
He didna mind a wheet;
Nor kent the derk'nin frae the daw,
The wulfire frae the weet;
Nor fuggage frae his feet.

His wife and weans frae time to time,
As they gaed by the cratur,
Wud haut to hae a gowk at him
And shak their pows, or natter:
'He's no like growin better.'

It maun be twenty year or mair
Sin thocht's been a' his trade:
And naebody can tell for shair
Whether this unco taed
Is dead, or thinks he's dead.

taed, toad; *atween*, between; *wheet*, whit; *derk'nin*, twilight; *daw*, dawn; *wulfire*,
summer lightning; *fuggage*, moss; *weans*, children; *cratur*, creature; *haut*, hop;
gowk, gape; *pows*, heads; *natter*, gossip; *shair*, sure; *unco*, extraordinary

SAMSON

The hands that riv'd the lion's maw,
The hands that wi' nae sword nor spear
Brocht a hale army to the fa'
Like it had been a field o' bear,
Were hankl'd be a lassie's hair.

Samson, wha brak a raip like straw,
And dung the doors o' Ashkelon;
Wha heistit Gaza's gates awa,
Becam the byword o' the toun —
Afore he pu'd the pillars doun.

riv'd, tore apart; *bear*, barley; *hankl'd*, entangled; *brak*, broke; *raip*, rope; *dung*, beat
down; *heistit*, hoisted; *byword*, proverbial example

JOSEPH MACLEOD

from THE MEN OF THE ROCKS

Our pastures are bitten and bare
our wool is blown to the winds
our mouths are stopped and dumb
our oatfields weak and thin.
Nobody fishes the loch
nobody stalks the deer.
Let us go down to the sea.
The friendly sea likes to be visited.

Our fathers sleep in the cemetery
their boats, cracked, by their side.
The sea turns round in his sleep
pleasure craft nod on the tide.
Sea ducks slumber on waves
Sea eagles have flown away.
Let us put out to sea.
The fat sea likes to be visited.

Fat sea, what's on your shelf?
all the grey night we wrestled.
To muscle, to skill, to petrol,
Hook oo rin yo! . . . one herring!
and of that only the head.
Dogfishes had the rest,
A parting gift from the sea.
The merry waves like to be visited.

Merry sea, what have you sent us?
A rusty English trawler?
The crew put into the hotel
the engineer overhauls her.

Gulls snatch offal to leeward.
We on the jetty await
gifts of the cod we can't afford . . .
The free sea likes to be visited.

Free were our father's boats
whose guts were strown on the shore.
Steam ships were bought by the rich
cheap from the last war.
They tear our nets to pieces
and the sea gives them our fishes.
Even he favours the rich.
The false sea likes to be visited.

A. D. MACKIE

SEA STRAIN

I fand a muckle buckie shell
    And held it to my lug,
And shurlan doun the stanie shore
    I heard the waters rug.
I heard the searchers at their wark,
    Waves wappan at the hull;
I heard, like some dementit sowl,
    The girnin o the gull.
I heard the reeshlin o the raip,
    I heard the timmers grane;
I heard the sab o a sailor's bride,
    Forever burd alane.

fand, found; *buckie*, convoluted shell; *lug*, ear; *shurlan*, murmuring; *rug*, drag;
wappan, wrestling; *sowl*, soul; *girnin*, complaining; *reeshlin*, rustling; *raip*, rope;
timmers, timbers; *grane*, groan; *burd alane*, absolutely alone

MOLECATCHER

Strampin' the bent, like the Angel o' Daith,
  The mowdie-man staves by;
Alang his pad the mowdie-worps
  Like sma' Assyrians lie.

And where the Angel o' Daith has been,
  Yirked oot o' their yirdy hames,
Lie Sennacherib's blasted hosts
  Wi' guts dung oot o' wames.

Sma' black tramorts wi' gruntles grey,
  Sma' weak weemin's han's,
Sma' bead-een that wid touch ilk hert
  Binnae the mowdie-man's.

strampin', trampling; *bent*, open field; *mowdie-man*, molecatcher; *pad*, path;
mowdie-worps, moles; *yirked*, jerked; *yirdy*, earthy; *dung*, knocked; *wames*, bellies;
tramorts, corpses; *gruntles*, snouts; *ilk*, each; *binnae*, except

WILLIAM MONTGOMERIE

ELEGY

for William Soutar, 1943

A narrowing of knowledge to one window
to a door swinging inward
on a man in a windless room
on a man inwardly singing
on a singing child
alone and never alone

a lonely child
singing
in a mirror dancing to a dancing child
memory sang
and words in a mimic dance
old words were young
and a child sang

A narrowing of knowledge to one room
to a doorway
to a door in a wall
swinging
bringing him friends
a narrowing of knowledge to
an arrow in bone
in the marrow
an arrow
death
strung on the string of the spine

To the live crystal in the palm
and the five fingers
to the slow thirty years' pearl in the hand
shelled in a skull
in the live face of a statue
sea-flowered on the neck of broken marble
sunk fourteen years in that aquarium.

ROBERT McLELLAN

SANG

There's a reid lowe in yer cheek,
Mither, and a licht in yer ee,
And ye sing like the shuilfie in the slae,
But no for me.

The man that cam the day,
Mither, that ye ran to meet,
He drapt his gun and fondlet ye
And I was left to greit.

Ye served him kail frae the pat,
Mither, and meat frae the bane.
Ye brocht him cherries frae the gean,
And I gat haurdly ane.

And nou he lies in yer bed,
Mither, and the licht growes dim,
And the sang ye sing as ye hap me ower
Is meant for him.

shuilfie, chaffinch; *slae*, sloe (blackthorn); *greit*, weep; *kail*, broth; *pat*, pot; *gean*, cherry-tree; *hap*, cover

J. K. ANNAND

FUR COATS

Said the whitrick to the stoat,
'I see ye've on your winter coat.
I dinna see the sense ava!
Ye're shairly no expectin snaw?'

To the whitrick said the stoat,
'At least it's mair nor you hae got.
I'm gled I dinna hae to wear
The same auld coat throughout the year.'

Said the whitrick to the stoat,
'I wadna mak owre muckle o't.
While nane will covet my auld coat
Your ermine fur wi tip o black
Will aiblins cleed a Provost's back.'

whitrick, weasel; *dinna*, don't; *ava*, at all; *shairly*, surely; *owrer muckle o't*, too much of it; *aiblins*, perhaps; *cleed*, clothe

SIC TRANSIT GLORIA MUNDI

*On viewing the remains of a clerical dignitary in a
medieval grave at Whithorn Priory.*

Aye, ye were a braw chiel aince!
Gowd ring on your fingur,
Jewelled cleik to hird your flock,
Nae dout a braw singer
When ye weet your whustle at the mass wi
Wine frae a siller-gilt tassie.

And look at ye nou!
Sax centuries, and the wecht
O sax fute o mools hae wrocht
A bonnie transformation
That hardly suits your station,
Crozier crookit and scruntit,
Chalice and paten duntit,
Hause-bane dwynit,
Harn-pan crynit,
Your chaft-blade ajee
Juist like a Campbell's,
But that couldna be!
In Candida Casa a Campbell
Has never held the see.

And thon chiel frae the Meenistry,
Thon archeological resurrectionist,
He'll meisure ye in your kist
And tak a likeness o ye
Wi infra-reid, or aiblins
Ultra-violet ye,
The scientists syne will get ye,
Wi gaga-coonter vet ye,
Jalousin what's your age.
In jaurs they'll catalyse ye,
Ettlin to analyse ye,
Sin that's nou aa the rage.

Syne when ye're tabulatit,
Recordit, and debatit,
And richtly written doun,
They'll set ye in a case
In thon Museum place
In Edinburgh Toun.

The folk that hear your fame
Will come on holiedays
And dress't in Sabbath claes
Mind ye on aulden days
And gar ye feel at hame.

aye, yes; *braw*, fine; *chiel*, fellow; *aince*, once; *cleik*, crook; *weet your whustle*, wet
your whistle; *siller*, silver; *tassie*, cup; *mools*, the grave; *scruntit*, scratched; *duntit*,
beaten; *hause-bane*, neck-bone; *dwynit*, wasted; *harn-pan*, skull; *crynit*, shrunken;
chaft-blade, jaw bone; *ajee*, awry; *Campbell*, crooked mouth; *kist*, chest; *aiblins*,
perhaps; *jalousin*, guessing; *ettlin*, intending; *sin*, since; *aa*, all; *claes*, clothes;
gar, make

GEORGE BRUCE

INHERITANCE

This which I write now
Was written years ago
Before my birth
In the features of my father.

It was stamped
In the rock formations
West of my hometown.
Not I write,

But, perhaps William Bruce,
Cooper,
Perhaps here his hand
Well articled in his trade.

Then though my words
Hit out
An ebullition from
City or flower

There not my faith,
These the paint
Smeared upon
The inarticulate,

The salt-crusted sea-boot,
The red-eyed mackerel,
The plate shining with herring,
And many men,

Seamen and craftsmen and curers,
And behind them
The protest of hundreds of years,
The sea obstinate against the land.

THE FISHERMAN

As he comes from one of those small houses
Set within the curve of the low cliff
For a moment he pauses
Foot on step at the low lintel
Before fronting wind and sun.
He carries out from within something of the dark
Concealed by heavy curtain,
Or held within the ship under hatches.

Yet with what assurance
The compact body moves,
Head pressed to wind,
His being at an angle
As to anticipate the lurch of earth.

Who is he to contain night
And still walk stubborn
Holding the ground with light feet
And with a careless gait?
Perhaps a cataract of light floods,
Perhaps the apostolic flame.
Whatever it may be
The road takes him from us,
Now the pier is his, now the tide.

LAOTIAN PEASANT SHOT

seen on television war report documentary

He ran in the living air,
exultation in his heels.

A gust of wind will erect
a twisting tower of dried leaves
that will collapse when
the breath is withdrawn.

He turned momentarily,
his eyes looking into his fear,
seeking himself.

When he fell the dust
hung in the air
like an empty container
of him.

AT THE LOCH OF STRATHBEG

Space! – here runs astringent air
Across the loch fixed
In three miles of flat,
The habitat of thistle and hare.

Outpaced gull and tern
Swing in a catspaw's fuff.
By the shocked occasional tree
Wind twists to the fern.

Cower weasel in the wall,
Look upon our scenery.
The loch fixed,
Tree torn from soil.

SUMBURGH HEID

Rummle an' dunt o' watter,
Blatter, jinkin, turn an' rin –
A' there – burst an' yatter,
Sea soun an' muckle an' sma win'
Heich in a lift clood-yokit.
Heich abune purpie sea, abune reid
Rocks – skraichs. That an' mair's i' the dirdit
Word – Sumburgh, Sumburgh Heid.

heid, head; *dunt*, impact; *blatter*, battering blow; *jinkin*, dodging; *yatter*, chatter; *heich*, high; *abune*, above; *purpie*, purple; *lift*, sky; *clood-yokit*, clouds linked together; *skraichs*, screeches; *dirdit*, buffeted

URN BURIAL
(I.M. Scots Tongue)

It wis hardly worth peying for
a casket
the body wis that peely-wally,

nae bluid in't
lukit like a
scrap o' broun paper

papyrus mebbe?
nae gran eneuch
for that,

but there wis some gran mourners, the
Editor o' the Scottish National Dictionary,
Heid o' the Depairtment o' Scot. Lit.,
President o' the Burns Federation,
President o' the Lallans Society,
President o' the Saltaire Society,
a' present in strict alphabetical order an'
ane/twa orra Scot. Nats.

Syne cam a fuff o' win'
an' liftit it oot o' the bowlie
an' hine awa,

a wee bird sang

Dew dreep'd
on the beld heids
o' the auld men
stude gloweran
at the tuim tomb.

'She's jinkit again,
the bitch!'
said the man wi' the spade.

peely-wally, sickly; *gran eneuch*, grand enough; *orra*, odd; *syne*, then; *fuff*, puff; *hine*, far; *dreep'd*, dripped; *beld*, bald; *tuim*, empty; *jinkit*, dodged

ROBERT GARIOCH

SISYPHUS

Bumpity doun in the corrie gaed whuddran the pitiless whun
    stane.
Sisyphus, pechan and sweitan, disjaskit, forfeuchan and
    broun'd-aff,
sat on the heather a hanlawhile, houpan the Boss didna spy
    him,
seean the terms of his contract includit nae mention of tea-
    breaks,
syne at the muckle big scunnersome boulder he trauchlit
    aince mair.
Ach, hou kenspeckle it was, that he ken'd ilka spreckle and
    blotch on't.
Heavan awa at its wecht, he manhaunnlit the bruitt up the
    brae-face,
takkan the easiest gait he had fand in a fudder of dour years,
hauddan awa frae the craigs had affrichtit him maist in his
    youth-heid,
feelan his years aa the same, he gaed cannily, tenty of slipped
    discs.
Eftir an hour and a quarter he warslit his wey to the brae's
    heid,

hystit his boulder richt up on the tap of the cairn – and it
 stude there!
streikit his length on the chuckie-stanes, houpan the Boss
 wadna spy him,
had a wee look at the scenery, feenisht a pic and a cheese-
 piece.
Whit was he thinkin about, that he jist gied the boulder a wee
 shove?
Bumpity doun in the corrie gaed whuddran the pitiless whun
 stane,
Sisyphus dodderan eftir it, shair of his cheque at the month's
 end.

corrie, mountain hollow; *gaed whuddran*, went rushing; *whun stane*, whinstone;
pechan, panting; *sweitan*, sweating; *disjaskit*, worn out; *forfeuchan*, exhausted;
broun'd-aff, browned-off; *hanlawhile*, short time; *syne*, then; *scunnersome*,
disgusting; *trauchlit*, struggled; *aince mair*, once more; *kenspeckle*, well-known;
spreckle, speckle; *wecht*, weight; *bruitt*, brute; *gait*, way; *fand*, found; *fudder*, large
number; *dour*, hard; *craigs*, rocks; *affrichtit*, frightened; *maist*, most; *gaed cannily*,
went carefully; *tenty*, wary; *warslit*, struggled; *streikit*, stretched; *chuckie-stanes*,
pebblestones; *dodderan eftir*, dawdling after

DID YE SEE ME?

I'll tell ye of ane great occasioun:
I tuke pairt in a graund receptioun.
Ye cannae hae the least perceptioun
hou pleased I was to get the invitatioun

tae assist at ane dedicatioun.
And richtlie sae; frae its inceptioun
the hale ploy was my ain conceptioun;
I was asked to gie a dissertatioun.

The functioun was held in the aipen air,
a peety, that; the keelies of the toun,
a toozie lot, gat word of the affair.

We cudnae stop it: they jist gaithert roun
to mak sarcastic cracks and grin and stare.
I wisht I hadnae worn my M.A. goun.

hale ploy, whole affair; *aipen*, open; *keelies*, louts; *toozie*, untidy

AND THEY WERE RICHT

I went to see 'Ane Tryall of Hereticks'
by Fiona MacColla, treatit as a play;
a wyce-like wark, but what I want to say
is mair taen-up wi halie politics

nor wi the piece itsel; the kinna tricks
the unco-guid get up til whan they hae
their wey. Yon late-nicht ploy on Setturday
was thrang wi Protestants and Catholics,

an eydent audience, wi fowth of bricht
arguments wad hae kept them gaun till Monday.
It seemed discussion wad last out the nicht,

hadna the poliss, sent by Mrs Grundy
pitten us out at twelve. And they were richt!
Wha daur debait religion on a Sunday?

wyce-like, intelligent-seeming; *taen-up*, concerned; *halie*, holy; *unco-guid*, all-too-good; *thrang*, crowded; *eydent*, eager; *fowth*, plenty; *gaun*, going

From GARIOCH'S REPONE TIL GEORGE BUCHANAN

In kep and goun, the new M.A.,
wi burnisht harns in bricht array
    frae aa the bukes he's read,
nou realises wi dismay
he's left it owre late in the day
    to learn anither tred.
What has he got that he can sell?
nae maitter tho he scrieve a fell
guid-gauan prose-style, Ethel M. Dell
    he canna rival.
Poetic pouers may win him praise
but guarantee nae fowth o days
    for his survival.
A kep and goun – what dae they
    maitter?
A kep and bells wad suit him better.
He's jist an orra human cratur,
    yaup as a lous.
Tho he be latinate and greekit,
he kens that ilka yett is steekit
    but Moray Hous.
Nou see him in his college blazer;
the Muse luiks on; it maun amaze her
    to see his tricks,
like shandy in the Galloway Mazer
or Occam tyauvan wi his razor
    to chop-up sticks.
Afore his cless he staunds and talks
or scrieves awa wi colour'd chalks;
nae mair by Helicon he walks,
    or e'en St Bernard's Well.

In clouds o blackbrod stour he's jowan
anent some aibstract plural noun,
while aa the time his hert is lowan
        in its wee private hell.
At nine a.m. she hears him blaw
his whustle, and lay doun the law
out in the pleygrund, whether snaw
        shoures doun, or Phoebus shines.
Wi muckle tyauve she sees him caa
chaos til order; raw by raw
he drills his bairns in mainner braw,
        weill covered-aff in lines.
They mairch til the assembly-haa
to sing a sang and hear a saw
or maybe jist a threit or twa
        as the heidmaister chuse.
Syne in his room she sees him faa
to wark; she hears him rant and jaw
and hoast and hawk and hum and haw,
blatter and blawp and bumm and blaw
and natter like a doited craw,
teachan his bairns to count and draw
and chant gizinties and Bee-baw,
and read and spell and aa and aa,
far owre taen-up wi maitters smaa
        to mind him of the Muse.
Whan schule has skailt, he maun awa,
whaur? ye may speir – to some green shaw
to meditate a poem? – Na!
        His lowsan-time is faur
aheid; to organise fi'baw
        and plouter in the glaur.

Late in the day he hirples hame
wi bizzan heid, a wee-thing lame,
and indisjeesters in his wame,
    and that may cause nae wunner;
the break spells duty, jist the same . . .
    to supervise schule-denner.
Sae ilka week and month and year
his life is tined in endless steir,
grindan awa in second-gear
    gin teaching be his fate.
The Muse, wha doesna share her rule
wi sordid maisters, leaves the fule,
    sans merci, til his fate.

MORAL
Lat onie young poetic chiel
that reads thae lines tak tent richt weill:
THINK TWICE, OR IT'S OWRE LATE!

kep, cap; *harns*, brains; *scrieve*, write; *fell*, very; *guid-gauan*, good-going; *fowth*,
plenty; *orra*, odd; *yaup*, hungry; *ilka yett*, every gate; *steekit*, shut fast; *Moray Hous*,
Edinburgh's teacher-training college; *tyauvan*, working hard; *stour*, dust; *jowan*,
ringing; *anent*, concerning; *lowan*, flaming; *bairns*, children; *faa*, fall; *hoast*, cough;
doitit craw, silly crow; *gizinties*, goes-intos (counting); *Bee-baw*, children's song;
owre taen-up, too occupied; *schule*, school; *skailt*, dispersed; *speir*, ask; *shaw*,
grove; *lowsan-time*, time to stop work; *fi'baw*, football; *plouter*, splash; *glaur*, mud;
hirples, limps; *wee-thing*, little; *indisjeesters*, indigestion; *wame*, stomach; *tined*,
lost; *gin*, if; *chiel*, fellow; *tak tent*, take care

BRITHER WORM

I saw a lang worm snoove throu the space atween twa stanes,
pokan his heid, if he had yin, up throu a hole in the New
    Toun,
up throu a crack ye wad hardly hae seen, in an area of stane,

unkenn'd uplifted tons of mason-wark piled on the soil,
wi causey-streets, biggit of granite setts, like blank waas flat
    on the grund,
plainstane pavements of Thurso slabs laid owre the stane-
    aircht cellars,
the area fifteen feet doun, wi weill-jyned flagstanes, Regency
    wark.
Nou, in my deeded stane-and-lime property, awntert a nesh
    and perfect worm.
I was abaysit wi thochts of what was gaun-on ablow my feet,
that the feued and rented grund was the soil of the naitural
    Drumsheuch Forest,
and that life gaed on thair in yon soil, and had sent out a spy,
thinkan some Friend of the Worms had slockent them wi a
    shoure,
whan I on my side of the crust had teemit twa-three pails of
    water,
meaning to scrub the place doun wi a besom I had jist bocht.
Sae a saft, soupple and delicate, pink and naukit craitur
neatly wan out frae atween thae dressed, weill-laid,
    unnaitural stanes.
I watched, and thocht lang of the ferlies of Naitur; I didna
    muve;
I thocht of the deeps of the soil, deeper nor the sea. I made
    nae sound.
A rat raxt frae a crack atween twa stanes.
I shuik wi sudden grue. He leukit at me, and wes gane.

snoove, move slowly and smoothly; *awntert*, ventured; *nesh*, delicate; *slockent*,
quenched thirst; *ferlies*, wonders; *grue*, horror

NEMO CANEM IMPUNE LACESSIT

I kicked an Edinbro dug-luver's dug,
leastweys I tried; my timing wes owre late.
It stopped whit it wes daein til my gate
and skelpit aff to find some ither mug.

Whit a sensation! If a clockwark thug
suid croun ye wi a brolly owre yir pate,
the Embro folk wad leave ye til yir fate;
it's you, maist like, wad get a flee in yir lug.

But kick the Friend of Man! Or hae a try!
The Friend of Wummin, even, that's faur waur
a felony, mair dangerous forbye.

Meddle wi puir dumb craiturs gin ye daur;
that maks ye a richt cruel bruitt, my! my!
And whit d'ye think yir braw front yett is for?

skelpit, moved quickly; *suid*, should; *lug*, ear; *forbye*, as well; *craiturs*, creatures;
yett, gate

NORMAN MacCAIG

EDINBURGH COURTYARD IN JULY

Hot light is smeared as thick as paint
On these ramshackle tenements. Stones smell
Of dust. Their hoisting into quaint
Crowsteps, corbels, carved with fool and saint,
Holds fathoms of heat, like water in a well.

Cliff-dwellers have poked out from their
High cave-mouths brilliant rags on drying-lines;
They hang still, dazzling in the glare,
And lead the eye up, ledge by ledge to where
A chimney's tilted helmet winks and shines.

And water from a broken drain
Splashes a glassy hand out in the air
That breaks in an unbraiding rain
And falls still fraying, to become a stain
That spreads by footsteps, ghosting everywhere.

ASSISI

The dwarf with his hands on backwards
Sat, slumped like a half-filled sack
On tiny twisted legs from which
Sawdust might run,
Outside the three tiers of churches built
In honour of St Francis, brother
Of the poor, talker with birds, over whom
He had the advantage
Of not being dead yet.

A priest explained
How clever it was of Giotto
To make his frescoes tell stories
That would reveal to the illiterate the goodness
Of God and the suffering
Of His Son. I understood
The explanation and
The cleverness.

A rush of tourists, clucking contentedly,
Fluttered after him as he scattered
The grain of the Word.

It was they who had passed
The ruined temple outside, whose eyes
Wept pus, whose back was higher
Than his head, whose lopsided mouth
Said *Grazie* in a voice as sweet
As a child's when she speaks to her mother
Or a bird's when it spoke
To St Francis.

NEGLECTED GRAVEYARD, LUSKENTYRE

I wade in the long grass,
Barking my shins on gravestones.
The grass overtops the dyke.
In and out of the bay hesitates the Atlantic.

A seagull stares at me hard
With a quarterdeck eye, leans forward
And shrugs into the air.
The dead rest from their journey from one wilderness to
     another.

Considering what they were,
This seems a proper disorder.
Why lay graves by rule
Like bars of a cage on the ground? To discipline the unruly?

I know a man who is
Peeped at by death. No place is
Atlantics coming in;
No time but reaches out to touch him with a cold finger.

He hears death at the door.
He knows him round every corner.
No matter where he goes
He wades in long grass, barking his shins on gravestones.

The edge of the green sea
Crumples. Bees are in clover.
I part the grasses and there —
Angus MacLeod, drowned. Mary his wife. Together.

SOUNDS OF THE DAY

When a clatter came,
it was horses crossing the ford.
When the air creaked, it was
a lapwing seeing us off the premises
of its private marsh. A snuffling puff
ten yards from the boat was the tide blocking and
unblocking a hole in a rock.
When the black drums rolled, it was water
falling sixty feet into itself.

When the door
scraped shut, it was the end
of all the sounds there are.

You left me
beside the quietest fire in the world.

I thought I was hurt in my pride only,
forgetting that,
when you plunge your hand in freezing water,
you feel
a bangle of ice round your wrist
before the whole hand goes numb.

BYRE

The thatched roof rings like heaven where mice
Squeak small hosannahs all night long,
Scratching its golden pavements, skirting
The gutter's crystal river-song.

Wild kittens in the world below
Glare with one flaming eye through cracks,
Spurt in the straw, are tawny brooches
Splayed on the chests of drunken sacks.

The dimness becomes darkness as
Vast presences come mincing in,
Swagbellied Aphrodites, swinging
A silver slaver from each chin.

And all is milky, secret, female.
Angels are hushed and plain straws shine.
And kittens miaow in circles, stalking
With tail and hindleg one straight line.

COUNTRY DANCE

The room whirled and coloured
and figured itself with dancers.
Another gaiety seemed born of theirs
and flew like streamers
between their heads and the ceiling.

I gazed, coloured and figured,
down the tunnel of streamers –
and there, in the band, an old fiddler
sawing away in the privacy
of music. He bowed lefthanded and his right hand
was the wrong way round. Impossible.
But the jig bounced, the gracenotes
sparkled on the surface of the tune.
The odd man out, when it came to music,
was the odd man in.

There's a lesson here, I thought, climbing
into the pulpit I keep in my mind.
But before I'd said Firstly brethren, the tune
ended, the dancers parted, the old fiddler
took a cigarette from the pianist, stripped off
the paper and ate the tobacco.

HIGHLAND FUNERAL

Over the dead man's house, over his landscape
the frozen air was a scrawny psalm
I believed in, because it was pagan
as he was.

Into it the minister's voice
spread a pollution of bad beliefs.
The sanctimonious voice dwindled away
over the boring, beautiful sea.

The sea was boring, as grief is,
but beautiful, as grief is not.
Through grief's dark ugliness I saw that beauty
because he would have.

And that darkened the ugliness . . . Can the dead
help? I say so. Because, a year later,
that sanctimonious voice is silent and the pagan
landscape is sacred in a new way.

QUEEN OF SCOTS

Mary was depressed.
She hadn't combed her red hair yet.
She hadn't touched her frightful Scottish breakfast.
Her lady-in-waiting, another Mary,
had told Rizzio Her Majesty wasn't at home,
a lie so obvious it was another way
of telling the truth.

Mary was depressed.
She wanted real life and here she was
acting in a real play, with real blood in it.
And she thought of the years to come
and of the frightful plays that would be written
about the play she was in.

She said something in French
and with her royal foot she kicked
the spaniel that was gazing at her
with exophthalmic adoration.

TOAD

Stop looking like a purse. How could a purse
squeeze under the rickety door and sit,
full of satisfaction, in a man's house?

You clamber towards me on your four corners —
one hand, one foot, one hand, one foot.

I love you for being a toad,
for crawling like a Japanese wrestler,
and for not being frightened.

I put you in my purse hand, not shutting it,
and set you down outside directly under
every star.

A jewel in your head? Toad,
you've put one in mine,
a tiny radiance in a dark place.

SORLEY MACLEAN

COIN IS MADAIDHEAN-ALLAIDH

Thar na sìorruidheachd, thar a sneachda,
chì mi mo dhàin neo-dheachdte:
chì mi lorgan an spòg a' breacadh
gile shuaimhneach an t-sneachda:

calg air bhoile, teanga fala,
gadhair chaola 's madaidhean-allaidh,
a' leum thar mullaichean nan gàradh,
a' ruith fo sgàil nan craobhan fàsail,
ag gabhail cumhang nan caol-ghleann,
a' sireadh caisead nan gaoth-bheann;
an langan gallanach a' sianail
thar loman cruaidhe nan àm cianail,
an comhartaich bhiothbhaun na mo chluasan,
an deann-ruith ag gabhail mo bhuadhan;
réis nam madadh 's nan con iargalt
luath air tòrachd na fhiadhaich,
troimh na coilltean gun fhiaradh,
thar mullaichean nam beann gun shiaradh;
coin chiùine cuthaich mo bhàrdachd,
madaidhean air tòir na h-àilleachd,
àilleachd an anama 's an aodainn,
fiadh geal thar bheann is raointean,
fiadh do bhòidhche ciùine gaolaich,
fiadhach gun sgur, gun fhaochadh.

DOGS AND WOLVES

Across eternity, across its snow, I see my unwritten poems: I see the spoor of their
paws dappling the august whiteness of the snow: bristles raging, bloody-tongued,
lean greyhounds and wolves, leaping over the dykes, running under the shade of the
trees of the wilderness, taking the narrow defile of glens, making for the steepness of
windy mountains; their baying yell shrieking across the hard bareness of the terrible
times, their everlasting barking in my ears, their hot onrush seizing my mind; career
of wolves and eery dogs, swift in pursuit of the quarry, through the forests without
veering, over the mountaintops without sheering; the mild mad dogs of my poetry,
wolves in chase of loveliness, loveliness of soul and face, a white deer over hills and
plains, the deer of your gentle beloved beauty, a hunt without halt, without respite.

KNIGHTSBRIDGE LIBIA AN ÒG-MHIOS 1942

Ged tha mi 'n diugh ri uchd a' bhatail
Chan ann an seo mo shac 's mo dhiachainn,
Cha ghunnachan 's cha thancan Roimeil,
Ach mo ghaol bhith coirbte briagach.

KNIGHTSBRIDGE, LIBYA, JUNE 1942

Though I am today against the breast of battle, not here my burden and my
extremity; not Rommel's guns and tanks, but that my darling should be depraved and
a liar.

REOTHAIRT

Uair is uair agus mi briste
thi mo smuain ort is tu òg,
is lìonaidh an cuan do-thuigsinn
le làn-mara 's mìle seòl.

Falaichear cladach na trioblaid
le bhodhannan is tiùrr a' bhròin
is buailidh an tonn gun bhristeadh
mu m' chasan le suathadh sròil.

Ciamar nach do mhair an reothairt
bu bhuaidhe dhomh na do na h-eòin,
agus a chail mi a cobhair
's i tràghadh boinn' air bhoinne bròin?

SPRINGTIDE

Again and again when I am broken my thought comes on you when you were young,
and the incomprehensible ocean fills with floodtide and a thousand sails.
The shore of trouble is hidden with its reefs and the wrack of grief, and the
unbreaking wave strikes about my feet with a silken rubbing.
How did the springtide not last, the springtide more golden to me than to the birds,
and how did I lose its succour, ebbing drop by drop of grief?

HALLAIG

'Tha tìm, am fiadh, an Coille Hallaig.'

Tha bùird is tàirnean air an uinncig
triomh 'm faca mi an Aird an Iar
's tha mo ghaol aig Allt Hallaig
'na craoibh bheithe, 's bha i riamh

eadar an t-Inbhir 's poll a' Bhainne,
thall 's a bhos mu Bhaile-Chùirn:
tha i 'na beithe, 'na calltuinn,
'na caorunn dhireach sheang ùir.

Ann Screapadal mo chinnidh,
far robh Tarmad 's Eachunn Mór,
th 'n nigheanan 's am mic 'nan coille
ag gabhail suas ri taobh an lóin.

Uaibhreach a nochd na coilich ghiuthais
ag gairm air mullach Cnoc an Rà,
dìreach an druim ris a' ghealaich —
chan iadsan coille mo ghràidh.

Fuirichidh mi ris a' bheithe
gus an tig i mach an Càrn,
gus am bi am bearradh uile
o Bheinn na Lice f' a sgàil.

Mura tig 's ann theàrnas mi a Hallaig
a dh' ionnsaigh sàbaid nam marbh,
far a bheil an sluagh a' tathaich,
gach aon ghinealach a dh' fhalbh.

Tha iad fhathast ann a Hallaig,
Clann Ghill-Eain 's Clann MhicLeoid,
na bh' ann ri linn Mhic Ghille-Chaluim:
chunnacas na mairbh beò –

na fir 'nan laighe air an liannaig
aig ceann gach taighe a bh' ann,
na h-igheanan 'nan coille bheithe,
dìreach an druim, crom an ceann.

Eadar an Leac is na Feàrnaibh
tha 'n rathad mór fo chòinnich chiuin,
's na h-igheanan 'nam badan sàmhach
a' dol a Chlachan mar o thùs.

Agus a' tilleadh as a' Chlachan,
á Suidhisnis 's á tir nam beò;
a chuile té òg uallach
gun bhristeadh cridhe an sgeòil.

O Alt na Feàrnaibh gus an fhaoilinn
tha soilleir an dìomhaireacd nam beann
chan eil ach coimhthional nan nighean
ag cumail na coiseachd gun cheann,

a' tilleadh a Hallaig anns an fheasgar,
anns a' chamhanaich bhalbh bheò,
a' lìonadh nan leathadan casa,
an gàireachdaich 'nam chluais 'n ceò,

's am bòidhche 'na sgleò air mo chridhe
mun tig an ciaradh air na caoil,
's nuair theàrnas grian air cùl Dùn Cana
thig peileir dian á gunna Ghaoil;

's buailear am fiadh a tha' na thuaineal
a' snòtach nan làraichean feòir;
thig reothadh air a shùil 'sa choille;
chan fhaighear lorg air fhuil ro m' bheò.

HALLAIG

'Time, the deer, is in the Wood of Hallaig.'

The window is nailed and boarded through which I saw the West and my love is at
the Burn of Hallaig a birch tree, and she has always been

between Inver and Milk Hollow, here and there about Baile-chuirn: she is a birch, a
hazel, a straight slender young rowan.

In Screapadal of my people, where Norman and Big Hector were, their daughters
and their sons are a wood going up beside the stream.

Proud tonight the pine cocks crowing on the top of Cnoc an Ra, straight their backs
in the moonlight – they are not the wood I love.

I will wait for the birch wood until it comes up by the Cairn, until the whole ridge
from Beinn na Lice will be under its shade.

If it does not, I will go down to Hallaig, to the sabbath of the dead, where the people
are frequenting, every single generation gone.

They are still in Hallaig, Macleans and MacLeods, all who were there in the time of
MacGille Chaluim: the dead have been seen alive –

the men lying on the green at the end of every house that was, the girls a wood of
birches, straight their backs, bent their heads.

Between the Leac and Fearns the road is under mild moss and the girls in silent
bands go to Clachan as in the beginning.

And return from Clachan, from Suisnish and the land of the living; each one young
and light-stepping, without the heartbreak of the tale.

From the Burn of Fearns to the raised beach that is clear in the mystery of the hills,
there is only the congregation of the girls keeping up the endless walk,

coming back to Hallaig in the evening, in the dumb living twilight, filling the steep
slopes, their laughter in my ears a mist,

and their beauty a film on my heart before the dimness comes on the kyles, and
when the sun goes down behind Dun Cana a vehement bullet will come from the
gun of Love;

and will strike the deer that goes dizzily, sniffing at the grass-grown ruined homes;
his eyes will freeze in the wood; his blood will not be traced while I live.

DOUGLAS YOUNG

SABBATH I THE MEARNS

The geans are fleuran whyte i the green Howe o the Mearns;
wastlan winds are blawan owre the Mownth's cauld glacks,
whaur the whaups wheep round their nesties among the fog
    and ferns;
and the ferm-touns stand gray and lown, ilk wi its yalla stacks.
The kirk is skailan, and the fowk in Sabbath stand o blacks
are doucely haudan hame til their denners wi the bairns,
the young anes daffan and auld neebours haean cracks.

Thon's bien and canty livin for auld-farrant fermer-fowk
wha wark their lives out on the land, the bonnie Laigh o
    Mearns.
They pleu and harra, saw and reap, clatt neeps and tattie-
    howk,
and dinna muckle fash theirsels wi ither fowk's concerns.
There's whiles a chyld that's unco wild, but sune the wildest
    learns
gin ye're nae a mensefu fermer-chiel ye's be naething but a
    gowk,
and the auld weys are siccar, auld and siccar like the sterns.

They werena aye like thon, this auld Albannach race,
whas stanes stand heich upo' the Mownth whaur the wild
    whaup caas.
Focht for libertie wi Wallace, luikit tyrants i the face,
stuid a siege wi leal Ogilvie for Scotland's king and laws,*

---

* Sir George Ogilvie of Barras held Dunnottar Castle, with Charles II's regalia inside,
  against the Cromwellian General Monk.

i the Whigs' Vaut o Dunnottar testified for Freedom's cause.
Is there onie Hope to equal the Memories o this place?
The last Yerl Marischal's deid, faan doun his castle waas.

geans, cherry-trees; *Howe*, Valley; *wastlan*, western; *cauld glacks*, cold ravines;
whaups, curlews; *wheep*, whistle; *fog*, moss; *lown*, quiet; *skailan*, dispersing;
doucely, sedately; *daffan*, toying amorously; *cracks*, conversations; *bien*, contented;
canty, pleasant; *auld-farrant*, old-fashioned; *Laigh*, Lowlands; *pleu*, plough; *clatt
neeps*, rake turnips; *tattie-howk*, dig potatoes; *fash*, bother; *chyld*, fellow; *unco*,
unusually; *mensefu*, respectable; *gowk*, fool; *siccar*, certain; *sterns*, stars; *thon*, that;
heich, high; *faan*, fallen

LAST LAUCH

The Minister said it wald dee,
the cypress buss I plantit.
But the buss grew til a tree,
naething dauntit.

It's growan, stark and heich,
derk and straucht and sinister,
kirkyairdie-like and dreich.
But whaur's the Minister?

buss, bush, *kirkyairdie-like*, appropriate to a churchyard; *dreich*, dreary

G. S. FRASER

LEAN STREET

Here, where the baby paddles in the gutter,
Here in the slaty greyness and the gas,
Here where the women wear dark shawls and mutter
A hasty word as other women pass,

Telling the secret, telling, clucking and tutting,
Sighing, or saying that it served her right,
The bitch! – the words and weather both are cutting
In Causewayend, on this November night.

At pavement's end and in the slaty weather
I stare with glazing eyes at meagre stone,
Rain and the gas are sputtering together
A dreary tune! O leave my heart alone,

O leave my heart alone, I tell my sorrows,
For I will soothe you in a softer bed
And I will numb your grief with fat to-morrows
Who break your milk teeth on this stony bread!

They do not hear. Thought stings me like an adder,
A doorway's sagging plumb-line squints at me,
The fat sky gurgles like a swollen bladder
With the foul rain that rains on poverty.

HOMETOWN ELEGY
(For Aberdeen in Spring)

Glitter of mica at the windy corners,
Tar in the nostrils, under blue lamps budding
Like bubbles of glass and blue buds of a tree,
Night-shining shopfronts, or the sleek sun flooding
The broad abundant dying sprawl of the Dee:
For these and for their like my thoughts are mourners
That yet shall stand, though I come home no more,
Gasworks, white ballroom, and the red brick baths
And salmon nets along a mile of shore,

Or beyond the municipal golf-course, the moorland paths
And the country lying quiet and full of farms.
This is the shape of a land that outlasts a strategy
And is not to be taken with rhetoric or arms.
Or my own room, with a dozen books on the bed
(Too late, still musing what I mused, I lie
And read too lovingly what I have read),
Brantome, Spinoza, Yeats, the bawdy and wise,
Continuing their interminable debate,
With no conclusion, they conclude too late,
When their wisdom has fallen like a grey pall on my eyes,
Syne we maun part, there sall be nane remeid –
Unless my country is my pride, indeed,
Or I can make my town that homely fame
That Byron has, from boys in Carden Place,
Struggling home with books to midday dinner,
For whom he is not the romantic sinner,
The careless writer, the tormented face,
The hectoring bully or the noble fool,
But, just like Gordon or like Keith, a name:
A tall, proud statue at the Grammar School.

GEORGE CAMPBELL HAY

GREY ASHES

Be canny o trampan on grey ashes;
they steer an' the air wins the hert o thaim.
In their hidden hert there derns the grieshoch,
an' oot o the grieshoch is born the flame.

Be canny, be canny o grey ashes
that ligg but reek i the airless bield.
Swing, wund, swing twa points – they are reekan;
swing three – an' the bleeze rins owre the field.

canny, careful; *steer*, stir; *derns*, hides; *grieshoch*, glowing embers; *ligg*, lie; *but*, without; *reek*, smoke; *bield*, shelter; *bleeze*, blaze

COLD COLD

Heich o,
braes that the green things brockit are clootit wi snaw,
mavis an' merle wi the spent sun hae socht awa
Sooth aye, for the birk is nae bield wi the drift ablow.

Cauld, alas,
the Nor' wind hunts the kairrie frae cairn tae cairn,
the scowry cratur drants owre soopit flats o airn,
whar the green rash dandlet its hacklet heid, an' the laverock
    was.

Sair, sair –
whar the gowd nuts bendit the boos the straucht rods stan!
What ails the grizzlet airts that they tak sic a pick tae this
    lan'?
Laggan was leafy; the snaw blins the sma birds there.

heich, high; *braes*, hills; *brockitt*, variegated; *clootit*, clothed; *mavis*, thrush; *merle*, blackbird; *birk*, birch; *bield*, shelter; *cauld*, cold; *kairrie*, carrion-crow; *scowry*, shabby; *cratur*, creature; *drants*, passes slowly; *soopit*, swept; *airn*, iron; *rash*, rush; *hacklet*, feathered; *laverock*, lark; *sair*, sore; *boos*, boughs; *airts*, directions (of weather)

BISEARTA

Chi mi rè geàrd na h-oidhe
dreòs air chrith 'na fhroidhneas thall air fàire,
a' clapail le a sgiathaibh,
a' sgapadh 's a' coaradh rionnagan na h-hàird' ud.

Shaoileadh tu gun cluinnte,
ge cian, o 'bhuillsgein ochanaich no caoineadh,
ràn corruich no gàir fuatha,
comhart chon cuthaich uaidh no ulfhairt fhaolchon,
gun ruigeadh drannd an fhòirneirt
o'n fhùirneis òmair iomall fhéin an t-saoghail;
ach sud a' dol an leud e
ri oir an speur an tosdachd olc is aognaidh.

C' ainm nochd a th' orra,
na sràidean bochda anns an sgeith gach uinneag
a lasraichean 's a deatach,
a sradagan is sgreadail a luchd thuinidh,
is taigh air thaigh 'ga reubadh
am broinn a chéile am brùchdadh toit a' tuiteam?
Is có an nochd tha 'g atach
am Bàs a theachd gu grad 'nan cainntibh uile,
no a' spàirn measg chlach is shailthean
air bhàinidh a' gairm air cobhair, is nach cluinnear?
Cò an nochd a phàidheas
sean chis àbhaisteach na fala cumant?

Uair dearg mar lod na h-àraich,
uair bàn mar ghile thràighte an eagail éitigh,
a' dìreadh 's uair a' teàrnadh,
a' sìneadh le sitheadh àrd 's a' call a mheudachd,

a' fannachadh car aitil
's ag at mar anail dhiabhhail air dhéinead,
an t-Olc 'na chridhe 's 'na chuisle,
chì mi 'na bhuillean a' sìoladh 's a' leum e.
Tha 'n dreòs 'na oillt air fàire,
'na fhàinne ròis is òir am bun nan speuran,
a' breugnachadh 's ag àicheadh
le shoillse sèimhe àrsaidh àrd nan reultan.

BIZERTA

I see during the night guard a blaze flickering, fringing the skyline over yonder, beating with its wings and scattering and dimming the stars of that airt.

You would think that there would be heard from its midst, though far away, wailing and lamentation, the roar of rage and the yell of hate, the barking of the dogs from it or the howling of wolves, that the snarl of violence would reach from yon amber furnace the very edge of the world; but yonder it spreads along the rim of the sky in evil ghastly silence.

What is their name tonight, the poor streets where every window spews its flame and smoke, its sparks and the screaming of its inmates, while house upon house is rent and collapses in a gust of smoke? And who tonight are beseeching Death to come quickly in all their tongues, or are struggling among stones and beams, crying in frenzy for help, and are not heard? Who tonight is paying the old accustomed tax of common blood?

Now red like a battlefield puddle, now pale like the drained whiteness of foul fear, climbing and sinking, reaching and darting up and shrinking in size, growing faint for a moment and swelling like the breath of a devil in intensity, I see Evil as a pulse and a heart declining and leaping in throbs. The blaze, a horror on the skyline, a ring of rose and gold at the foot of the sky, belies and denies with its light the ancient high tranquility of the stars.

PRIOSAN DA FHEIN AN DUINE?

Seall an t-amshan clis 'na shaighead
o' fhaire fo na neòil,
s an t-eun a' luasgan air a shlataig,
ag cur a bhith air fad 'na cheòl.

Their gnìomh is guth gach creutair ruinn,
ach éisdeachd riu air chòir:
'Cha chuir ceann is cridh' air iomrall thu.
Bi iomlan is bi beò.'

Cò air bith a chruthaich sinn,
cha d'rinn E'n cumadh ceàrr,
is mar thig air tùs gach duine
air bheag uireasbhuidh o 'làimh.
A bheil ni nach biodh air chomas da,
ach cothrom a thoirt dhà,
is a bhuadhan uile comhla ann
ag còrdach 'nan comfhàs?

Ach nì e tric de 'bhuadhanna
bròg chuagach fo 'shail,
cuid dhuibh fo'n chuip, gun srian riu,
is an dà thrian diubh 'nan tàmh.
Bidh an cridhe 'na thìoran aimhreiteach,
s an ceann aige 'na thràill,
no bidh an corp 'na phrìosanach,
s an inntinn air 'na geàrd.

Ceann is cridhe, teine s coinneal
a thoirt soluis duinn is blàiths,
an corp treun s an t-anam maothsgiathach
air aoigheachd ann car tràth,
fhuair sinn, s dà chois a shiubhal
gu ceart cunbhalach air làr,
is dà shùil a shealladh suas uaith,
no 'ruith cuairt nan ceithir àird.

An cridhe fialaidh misneachail,
na bu chiomach e am fròig,
ùraich cridh' an tsaoghail leis –
cuir mu sgaoil e – cuir gu stròdh.

Biodh do dhruim s do shealladh dìreach,
agus t'inntinn geur gun cheò;
lean gach beò a th'ann mar thiomnadh,
is bi iomlan is bi beò.

Is seall an triochshluagh dàicheil rianail,
nach robh riamh ach lethbheò,
is beachdan chàich 'nan gàradh-crìche dhaibh
'gan criònadh ann an crò.
Nigh snidhe mall an àbhaistich
an sgarlaid as an clò,
is thug e breacan ùr an nàduir
gus a' ghnàthach ghlas fadheòidh.

Ma's seabhag bhras no smeòrach thu,
mìn no ròmach clò do ghnè,
na dèan a' Chruitheachd a nàrachadh
le nàir' á cridhe s á cré.
Mar thaing do'n Tì 'chuir deò annad,
ma tha do dhòigh 'na Chreud,
no mar fhialachd do d'chomhdhaoine,
bi beò is bi thu fhéin.

MAN HIS OWN PRISON?

See the sudden gannet come as an arrow from his watching under the clouds, and the bird rocking on its branch, putting all its being into its music. The actions and voices of every creature say to us, if we would but listen to them rightly: 'Head and heart will not lead you astray. Be complete and be alive.'

Whoever it is has created us, His modelling was not at fault, to judge from how every man comes at first with few defects from His Hand. Is there anything that would not be within man's powers, were but the chance given to him, with all his qualities together harmonising in a united growth?

But often he makes of his qualities a lopsided shoe under his heel; some of them, unbridled, under the whip, and two-thirds of them in idleness. The heart may be a turbulent tyrant, with the head under it, its thrall; or the body may be a prisoner, with the intellect standing over it on guard.

Head and heart, fire and candle, to give us light and warmth; the strong body, and the soul with its delicate wings a guest in it for a while – we have that, and two feet to travel right firmly on the ground; with two eyes to look up from it, or to run the circle of the four airts.

The generous, spirited heart, let it not crouch, a prisoner, in a nook. Freshen the heart of the world with it. Unleash it. Be spendthrift with it. Let your back and your gaze be straight, and your mind keen and unmisted; follow the witness of every living thing there is, and be complete and be alive.

And see the plausible orderly dwarf-people, who were never but half living, with the opinions of others as a march-dyke round them, wasting them away in a pen. The slow seeping of the habitual has washed the scarlet out of their cloth, and reduced the fresh tartan of their natures to the grey customary at length.

Whether you are a headlong hawk or a thrush, smooth or shaggy the stuff of your character, do not put Creation to shame by being ashamed of heart and body. In thankfulness to the One who put breath in you (if your trust is in His Creed), or in generosity to your fellow men, be alive and be yourself.

SYDNEY GOODSIR SMITH

SWEIT HAIRT . . .

Sweit hairt, they say they greit for us –
Luve sae possessed can but destroy.
– But tell me why their een grow saft
As we pass by?

greit, weep; *een*, eyes

SPRING IN THE BOTANIC GARDENS

The trees are heavy with blossom –
And yet
As licht and lichtsome
As the birds that din,
Compete,
And fill all trees,
All licht,

With lustful chatter
Dartin, fidgin —
For the ae live thing is livin.

Here I sit amang it aa,
Aa this blythful ignorance
— Or iggorant blythfulness —
Of lust and generation,
The sap and sang of protected things,
Sitting here in the park bink,
Alane
— yet no aa that alane.
The lovers airm in airm amang the trees
Bear seelie witness to a numen here:
All here is her and here she is allwhar —
But whar?
Quick — look!
Nane marks or mocks
The viewless vision fleein by
Naked white feet on the gress —
It was a dream of love, maybe,
The drowsy bard, rapt, in some ither
Paradiesgartlein.

What wad ye hae, then?
Misery? Joy?
There's millions stairvin owre the yerth,
There's thousands fechtin for nocht that they believe —
I sit here in peace.
A wee speug, fearless, pecks at my fuit.
Ah love, count thy blessings!
Ay —

But all's dependent on anither's strength.

fidgin, moving restlessly; *ae*, one; *blythful*, merry; *bink*, bench; *seelie*, innocent; *allwhar*, everywhere; *yerth*, earth; *wee speug*, tiny sparrow; *fuit*, foot; *ay*, yes

THE KENLESS STRAND

My sails by tempest riven
The sea a race
Whaur suld be lown and lither
Aa's dispeace.

Dispeace o hairt that visions
Reefs it downa ride,
Dispeace o mind in rapids
Nane can guide:

And aye a face afore me
And anither face,
Ane luve's ancient tragedy
And ane its peace.

Here, on luve's fludetide I run
There, the unkent strand
Abune, the seamaws' tireless grief
Ayont, nae hyne, nae end.

kenless strand, boundless shore; *riven*, torn; *lown*, calm; *lither*, idleness; *downa*, dare not; *aye*, always; *ane*, one; *fludetide*, floodtide; *unkent*, unknown; *abune*, above; *seamaws*, seagulls; *ayont*, beyond; *hyne*, haven

LATE

Sweet hairt, I lay in bed last nicht
Alane and yet wi ye
Alane I lay but no my lane
For the lane bed was full o ye.

Aa kens there's whiles a silly truth
Sets in the drunkard's ee —
Here nou 's a forest-bleezan truth
Frae the hairt o the barley bree:
Its flame inflames the tither flame
As ye, and me . . .

We ken the flame inflames the flame
As the wind brings in the sea —
Ken, tae, that fire consumes itsel
— As ye, and me.

my lane, alone; *kens*, knows; *ee*, eye; *bleezan*, blazing; *barley bree*, whisky; *tither*, the other; *tae*, too

BROODING REBUKED

Wha by takkin thocht
A cubit gains?
Or liftin airms aloft
Can stop the rains?

Wha by tricksickolatrie
Wins a new sel?
Or girnin at his weird
Flee's ain hell?

I ken o nane that did
Sanct or ye or me —
The lesson o the hevins reads
Juist be.

takkin thocht, taking thought; *airms*, arms; *sel*, self; *girnin*, snarling; *weird*, fate; *flee's*, fly his; *ain*, own; *sanct*, saint

I SAW THE MUNE

I saw the mune at nune the day
Blue sky and sun and the mune there tae
It was the morning and the evening baith thegither
It's aye the morning and the eening baith thegither
   — For us.

At the last day
As at the first.
     But this, hairtbeat,
     Is bang in the middle
     And wants nae bush —
     Nae mair nor gowden wine does
     Or a broch around the mune
        That says

. . . Rain . . . rain . . .
Rain, beat doun
And raise the gowden corn again;
Sun, sheen on, all orient,
First day and last;
Mune, sheen —
The mornin and the eening baith thegither.

In the rule o the sun brairs the corn,
Sweys in the souch o the wind
Like the souch o the swaw in the faur-aff sea.
The mune ascendant —
Her dominion there . . . Sclanna!

Venus . . . Ceres . . . Pluvius . . .
    Names, juist names —
Sol and Luna there conjoined
    — Juist names.
        Names.

But though we name auld names, my maisters,
Calling the past to clout wir raggit coats
And decorate a platitude auld when God was a laddie,
Think nocht tis idle sherbet that we sup
In this Sicilian idolatrie –

Aa kens, nae need here to repeat,
There's millions on the earth has gods nor meat;
Thousands ligg in chains and need
For nocht but speakin freedom's leid.
In aa this waesomeness and want
Guilt for love were piddling cant.
Act, gin ye will, act and move!
But speak nae word except ye love
Or humbug, let me see ye staund
And cast the first stane frae your haund.

Here we love, remote and safe,
And cry that love is unity –
As lovers think they hae it baith
Though the earth quags beneath their feet.

I saw the mune at nune the day,
Blue sky and sun –
     A memorie.

mune, moon; *nune*, noon; *the day*, to-day; *tae*, too; *thegither*, together; *nae mair*, no more; *gowden*, golden; *broch*, halo; *sheen*, shine; *brairs*, sprouts; *sweys*, sways; *souch*, sigh; *swaw*, wave; *faur-aff*, far-off; *wir*, our; *laddie*, young boy; *ligg*, lie; *leid*, language; *waesomeness*, woefulness; *gin*, if; *quags*, shakes like a quagmire.

T. S. LAW

THE ROCKET

Man, it was an awfielik slaister o troke i the gairden the-day,
auld tin cans, a rickle o sticks, an yle-drum, pats
an pans, an a fankle o cavie wire lik the turrivees
o a surrealist gane wuid wi a bunnetfou o bees
hotterin ower the byke o his brain. *Noo, whit dae ye say
that is, son?* said I tae the young engineer. *Oh, that's
a rocket, daddie,* said the bairn wi een like the full
muin. Truith, but lukin at him, ma ain een were geyan dull.

Raxin for the starns, it's caad, the same auld stent
ilk generation has wrocht wi its pickle mair,
faither tae son, and i the end faur less nor was kent
o the starns his mither fund and I, whan there
was wonder atween us like the muin tae pree,
gey like the wonder in oor laddie's ee.

awfielik, awful; *slaister*, miscellany; *troke*, rubbish; *fankle*, entanglement; *cavie*,
hen-coop; *turrivees*, commotions; *wuid*, mad; *hottering*, simmering; *byke*, bees' nest;
geyan, extremely; *raxin*, reaching out; *starns*, stars; *stent*, fixed task; *wrocht*,
wrought; *pickle*, small portion; *pree*, experience

IMPORTANCE

He daesnae juist drap a name
or set it up and say grace wi 't,
he lays it oot on his haun
and hits ye richt in the face wi 't.

Generous tho, tae a faut.
Ay, no a ticht man, no mean wi 't.
Gie him anither chance
and he'll hit ye atween the een wi 't.

faut, fault; *ticht*, tight; *een*, eyes

W. S. GRAHAM

NIGHT'S FALL UNLOCKS THE DIRGE OF THE SEA

Night's fall unlocks the dirge of the sea
To pour up from the shore and befriending
Gestures of water waving, to find me
Dressed warm in a coat of land in a house
Held off the drowned by my blood's race
Over the crops of my step to meet some praise.

The surge by day by night turns lament
And by this night falls round the surrounding
Seaside and countryside and I can't
Sleep one word away on my own for that
Grief sea with a purse of pearls and debt
Wading the land away with salt in his throat.

By this loud night traded into evidence
Of a dark church of voices at hand
I lie, work of the gruff sea's innocence
And lie, work of the deaths I find
On the robbed land breathing air and
The friendly thief sea wealthy with the drowned.

From THE NIGHTFISHING

We are at the hauling then hoping for it
The hard slow haul of a net white with herring
Meshed hard. I haul, using the boat's cross-heave
We've started, holding fast as we rock back,
Taking slack as we go to. The day rises brighter
Over us and the gulls rise in a wailing scare
From the nearest net-floats. And the unfolding water
Mingles its dead.

Now better white I can say what's better sighted,
The white net flashing under the watched water,
The near net dragging back with the full belly
Of a good take certain, so drifted easy
Slow down on us or us hauled up upon it
Curved in a garment down to thicker fathoms.
The hauling nets come in sawing the gunwales
With herring scales.

The air bunches to a wind and roused sea-cries.
The weather moves and stoops high over us and
There the forked tern, where my look's whetted on distance,
Quarters its hunting sea. I haul slowly
Inboard the drowning flood as into memory,
Braced at the breathside in my net of nerves.
We haul and drift them home. The winds slowly
Turn round on us and

Gather towards us with dragging weights of water
Sleekly swelling across the humming sea
And gather heavier. We haul and hold and haul
Well the bright chirpers home, so drifted whitely
All a blinding garment out of the grey water.
And, hauling hard in the drag, the nets come in,
The headrope a sore pull and feeding its brine
Into our hacked hands.

Over the gunwale over into our deep lap
The herring come in, staring from their scales,
Fruitful as our deserts would have it out of
The deep and shifting seams of water. We haul
Against time fallen ill over the gathering
Rush of the sea together. The calms dive down.
The strident kingforked airs roar in their shell.
We haul the last

Net home and the last tether off the gathering
Run of the started sea. And then was the first
Hand at last lifted getting us swung against
Into the homing quarter, running that white grace
That sails me surely ever away from home.
And we hold into it as it moves down on
Us running white on the hull heeled to light.
Our bow heads home

Into the running blackbacks soaring us loud
High up in open arms of the towering sea.
The steep bow heaves, hung on these words, towards
What words your lonely breath blows out to meet it.
It is the skilled keel itself knowing its own
Fathoms it further moves through, with us there
Kept in its common timbers, yet each of us
Unwound upon

By a lonely behaviour of the all common ocean.
I cried headlong from my dead. The long rollers,
Quick on the crests and shirred with fine foam,
Surge down then sledge their green tons weighing dead
Down on the shuddered deck-boards. And shook off
All that white arrival upon us back to falter
Into the waking spoil and to be lost in
The mingling world.

MAURICE LINDSAY

GLASGOW NOCTURNE

Materialised from the flaked stones of buildings
dank with neglect and poverty, the pack,
thick-shouldered, slunk through rows of offices
squirting anonymous walls with their own lack .

of self-identity. Tongs ya bass, Fleet,
Fuck the Pope spurted like blood: a smear
protesting to the passing daylight folk
the prowled-up edge of menace, the spoor of fear

that many waters cannot quench, or wash
clean from what hands, what eyes, from what hurt hearts?
O Lord! the preacher posed at the park gates,
what must we do to be whole in all our parts?

Late on Saturday night, when shop fronts doused
their furniture, contraceptives, clothes and shoes,
violence sneaked out in banded courage,
bored with hopelessness that has nothing to lose.

A side-street shadow eyed two lovers together;
he, lured from the loyalties of the gang
by a waif who wore her sex like a cheap trinket;
she, touched to her woman's need by his wrong

tenderness. On the way from their first dance,
the taste of not enough fumbled their search
of hands and lips endeared in a derelict close.
Over the flarepath of their love, a lurch

thrust from the shadow, circling their twined bodies.
It left them clung before its narrowing threat
till she shrieked. They peeled her from her lover,
a crumpled sob of a doll dropped in the street,

while he received his lesson: ribs and jaw
broken, kidneys and testicles ruptured, a slit
where the knife licked his groin. Before he died
in the ambulance, she'd vanished. Shops lit

up their furniture, contraceptives, clothes and shoes
again. Next morning, there was a darker stain
than Tongs ya bass and Fleet on the edge of the kerb;
but it disappeared in the afternoon rain.

AT HANS CHRISTIAN ANDERSEN'S BIRTHPLACE, ODENSE, DENMARK

Sunlight folds back pages of quiet shadows
against the whitewashed walls of his birthplace. Tourists
    move
through crowded antiseptic rooms and ponder
what row after row of glass-cased papers ought to prove.

Somehow the long-nosed gangling boy who was only
at home in fairyland, has left no clues.
The tinder-box of Time we rub
answers us each the way we choose.

For kings have now no daughters left for prizes.
Swineherds must remain swineherds; and no spell
can make the good man prince; psychiatrists
have dredged up wonder from the wishing well.

The whole of his terrible, tiny world might be
dismissed as a beautiful madman's dream, but that each of us
    knows
whenever we move out from the warmth of our loneliness
we may be wearing the Emperor's new clothes.

AN ELEGY
(*Matthew Lindsay*: 1884–1969)

You might have died so many kinds of death
as you drove yourself through eighty-four Novembers –

1916. The Cameronian officer
keeping the Lewis gun he commanded chattering
over the seething mud, that the enemy
should be told only in terms of bulky bodies,
for which, oak leaves, a mention in dispatches.

1918. The fragment of a shell
leaving one side of a jaw and no speech,
the bone graft from the hip. Shakespeare mouthed
(most of the others asserting silences)
over and over again, till the old words
shaped themselves into audibility.

1921. An eighty-per-cent
disability pension, fifty the limit of life
expectancy, a determination of courage
that framed the public man, the ready maker
of witty dinner speeches, the League of Nations,
the benefits of insurance, the private man
shut in his nightly study, unapproachable,
sufficient leader of sporting tournaments,
debates, and the placing of goodwill greetings in clubs.

1935. Now safely past
the doctor's prophecies. Four children, a popular
outward man wearing maturity,
top of his business tree, when the sap falters
and the soon-to-be-again confounded doctors
pronounce a world-wide cruise the only hope,
not knowing hope was all he ever needed
or counted on to have to reckon with.

1940 to 50. Wartime fears
not for himself but for his family,
the public disappointments and the private
disasters written off with stock quotations
from Shakespeare or Fitzgerald, perhaps to prove
the well-known commonness of experience,
the enemy across the mud, old age.

1959. It was necessary
at seventy-five, to show he couldn't be taken
by enfilading weaknesses. A horse
raised his defiance up. It threw him merely
to Russia on a stretcher, with two sticks
to lean beginner's Russian upon.

1969. The end of a decade
of surgeons, paling blindness, heart attacks
all beaten with familiar literature
bent into philosophic platitudes,
to the January day in his dressing-gown
when he sat recording plans for a last Burns Supper —

You might have died so many kinds of death
as you drove yourself through eighty-four Novembers
till you fell from your bed, apologised for such foolishness,
and from your sleep rode out where no man goes.

AT THE MOUTH OF THE ARDYNE

The water rubs against itself,
glancing many faces at me.
One winces as the dropped fly
Tears its tension. Then it heals.

Being torn doesn't matter.
The water just goes on saying
all that water has to say:
what the dead come back to.

Then a scar opens.
Something of water is ripped out,
a struggle with swung air.
I batter it on a loaf of stone.

The water turns passing faces,
innumerable pieces of silver.
I wash my hands, pack up, and go
home wishing I hadn't come.

Later, I eat my guilt.

INFINITY

Gin I was Betelgeuse
birlan awa up there
frae the first, reid flichter o time
tae the end o evermair
I wudna be lanesome, whiles,
for the stairns, the sun an the mune
'ud be whinneran, lik masel,
till the whang o the Lord wore dune.

birlan, whirling; *flichter*, flicker; *whiles*, sometimes; *stairns*, stars; *whinneran*,
passing softly with a humming sound; *whang*, whip-lash

ROOTS

I brought a water-pitcher up from Spain,
guarding it on the 'plane
between my feet. It looked like shaped rest,
curves that much living-with had stressed
skin-brown; a woman's breasts, full gourdes
cool with what darkness hoards.

I've brought it to a lean and hating town,
to set it in the stillness of a room
where love is made; moistened, raised out of clay
to which alike, one day,
pitcher and flesh must both again go down.

TOWARD LIGHT

The distant fog-horns bicker, the near ones boom;
light bats across the ceiling of the room
where, forty years ago, I watched, awake;
a still unfocused schoolboy trying to take
life by the meaning. Then, the mist that gripped
the perfumed garden, kept the sea tight-lipped,
hung vague on sheltering curtains; the boy's mind
compassed on ships whose fogs lay far behind.
Now, with the frame loose, the window bare,
a blunt beam's thrown back on its own stare.

REVISITING INNELLAN

Sheltered behind a rock a woman sits
keeping an eye on more than what she knits;
her hands the flashing motion of the sea,
veined with the dulse of vulnerability.

Gulls, stiff as saddles, ride the little bay
much as they rode the winds of yesterday.
A toy yacht arrows over shallow water
wafted by splashing knees and yells of laughter.
The boy beside the pool lets down his hand
to guddle baby crabs from shifting sand.

The same reflected sky, the same blue shout
through which a bather plunges, and runs out,
his sticky skin rubbed dry with towelled grit,
a gravelly biscuit for his chittering bit.
Though different the clothes, the cut of ships,
the waves still curl those same contemptuous lips
that spit the wrack of winter up the beach,
lost purposes unshaped from human reach.

Watching alone, an old man nobody knows
catches inquiring looks, gets up and goes.

TOM SCOTT

BRAND THE BUILDER

On winter days, aboot the gloamin hour,
When the nock on the college touer
Is chappan lowsin-time,
And ilka mason packs his mell and tools awa
Under his banker, and bien forenenst the waa
The labourer haps the lave o the lime
Wi soppan sacks, to keep it frae a frost, or faa
o suddent snaw
Duran the nicht;

When scrawnie craws flap in the shell-green licht
Towards yon bane-bare rickle o trees
That heeze
Up on the knowe abuin the toun,
And the red goun
Is happan mony a student frae the snell nor-easter,
Malcolm Brand, the maister,
Seean the last hand throu the yett
Afore he bars and padlocks it,
Taks yae look aroond his stourie yaird
Whaur chunks o stane are liggan
Like the ruins o some auld-farrant biggin;
Picks a skelf oot o his baerd,
Scliffs his tacketty buits, and syne
Clunters hamelins doun the wyn'.

Doun by the sea
Murns the white swaw owre the wrack ayebydanlie.

The main street echoes back his fuitfaas
Frae its waas
Whaur owre the kerb and causeys, yellow licht
Presses back the mirk nicht
As shop fronts flude the pavin-stanes in places
Like the peintit faces whures pit on, or actresses,
To please their different customers.

Aye the nordren nicht, cauld as rumour
Taks command,
Chills the toun wi his militarie humour,
And plots his map o starns wi felloun hand.

Alang the shore
the greenan white sea-stallions champ and snore.

Stoopan throu the anvil pend
Gaes Brand,
And owre the coort wi the twa-three partan-creels,
The birss air fu
o the smell o the sea, and fish, and meltit glue;
Draws up at his door, and syne,
Hawkan his craig afore he gangs in ben,
Gies a bit scart at the grater wi his heels.

The kail-pat on the hob is hotteran fu
Wi the usual hash o Irish stew,
And by the grate, a red-haired bewtie frettit thin,
His wife is kaain a spurtle roond.
He swaps his buits for his baffies but a soond.

The twa-three bairns ken to mak nae din
When faither's in,
And sit on creepies roond aboot.
Brand gies a muckle yawn
And howks his paper oot.

Tither side the fire
The kettle hums and mews like a telephone wire.

> 'Lord, for what we are about to receive
> Help us to be truly thankful – Aimen:
> Woman ye've pit ingans in't again!'

> 'Gac wa, ye coorse auld hypocrite,
> Thank the Lord for your meat syne grue at it!'

Wi chowks drawn ticht in a speakless sconner
He glowers on her,
Syne on the quate and strecht-faced bairns:
Faulds his paper doun aside his eatin-airns
And, til the loud tick-tockin o the nock
Sups, and reads wi nae other word nor look.

The warld ootside
Like a lug-held seashell, sings wi the rinnan tide.

The supper owre, Brand redds up for the nicht.
Aiblins there's a schedule for to price
Or somethin nice
On at the picters – secont hoose –
Or some poleetical meetin wants his licht,
Or aiblins, wi him t-total aa his life
And no able to seek a pub for relief frae the wife,
Daunders oot the West Sands 'on the loose'.
Whitever tis,
The waater slorps frae his elbuck as he synds his phiz.

And this is aa the life he kens there is?

gloamin, twilight; *nock*, clock; *chappan*, striking; *lowsin*, stopping; *bien*, comfortable; *haps*, covers; *lave*, remainder; *rickle*, loose stack; *heeze*, heave; *knowe*, knoll; *snell*, sharp; *yett*, gate; *stourie*, dusty; *liggan*, lying; *auld-farrant biggin*, old-fashioned building; *skelf*, splinter; *hamelins*, homewards; *greinan*, yearning; *owsen*, oxen; *swaw*, wave; *ayebydanlie*, forever; *pend*, lane; *partan*, crab; *birss*, sharp; *hawkan his craig*, clearing his throat; *hotteran fu*, simmering full; *kaain*, turning; *spurtle*, porridge stick; *baffies*, slippers; *but*, without; *ingans*, onions; *grue*, be revolted; *chowks*, cheeks; *speakless sconner*, speechless disgust; *eatin-airns*, cutlery; *lug*, ear; *redds*, tidies; *aiblins*, perhaps; *daunders*, strolls; *slorps*, runs off; *synds his phiz*, washes his face

WILLIAM J. TAIT

NAE EXCUSE

I had been sae lang athirst,
Dowf an disjaskit in dry launds and laich,
Whan on the mountain peak she brocht me wine,
My haund it tremblit an ower-cowped the quaich.

dowf, dull; *disjaskit*, worn out; *laich*, low; *ower-cowped*, knocked over; *quaich*, drinking-vessel

THE RIGHT TRUE END OF LOVE?

I

Ilk dad the door gies,
My hairt gies anither.
Ilk stound my hairt gies,
Somewhaur a board 'll crack.
Nae hoose is vod till
The ghaists aa thrang thegither.
Wha kens what licht is
Till the warld 's dark?

II

Nicht-lang the day drees
Life gane dowf an dozent.
Life-lang the nicht dees
An the last ghaist turns its back.
Nae hairt is vod while
Pain still hauds open hoose in't:
But wha kens what licht is
Whan the warld 's dark?

ilk dad, each knock; *gies*, gives; *stound*, pang; *vod*, empty; *thegither*, together; *drees*, endures; *dowf*, dull; *dozent*, stupid

TIMOR MORTIS . . .

My son's guidfaither dees. I never kent him,
But feel fell sorry for his wife and bairns,
Mair sae that bairn I think on as my ain;
Yet tho I deem my dule 's for her alane,
Isnae the wirm that 's chawan at my harns:
Hou lang will *her* guidfaither be ahent him?

guidfaither, father-in-law; *dule*, sorrow; *harns*, brain

EDWIN MORGAN

KING BILLY

Grey over Riddrie the clouds piled up,
dragged their rain through the cemetery trees.
The gates shone cold. Wind rose
flaring the hissing leaves, the branches
swung, heavy, across the lamps.
Gravestones huddled in drizzling shadow,
flickering streetlight scanned the requiescats,
a name and an urn, a date, a dove
picked out, lost, half regained.
What is this dripping wreath, blown from its grave
red, white, blue, and gold
'To Our Leader of Thirty years Ago' —

Bareheaded, in dark suits, with flutes
and drums, they brought him here, in procession
seriously, King Billy of Brigton, dead,
from Bridgeton Cross: a memory of violence,
brooding days of empty bellies,
billiard smoke and a sour pint,
boots or fists, famous sherrickings,
the word, the scuffle, the flash, the shout,
bloody crumpling in the close,
bricks for papish windows, get
the Conks next time, the Conks ambush
the Billy Boys, the Billy Boys the Conks till
Sillitoe scuffs the razors down the stank —
No, but it isn't the violence they remember
but the legend of a violent man
born poor, gang-leader in the bad times
of idleness and boredom, lost in better days,

a bouncer in a betting club,
a quiet man at last, dying
alone in Bridgeton in a box bed.
So a thousand people stopped the traffic
for the hearse of a folk hero and the flutes
threw 'Onward Christian Soldiers' to the winds
from unironic lips, the mourners kept
in step, and there were some who wept.

Go from the grave. The shrill flutes
are silent, the march dispersed.
Deplore what is to be deplored,
and then find out the rest.

THE STARLINGS IN GEORGE SQUARE

I

Sundown on the high stonefields!
The darkening roofscape stirs –
thick – alive with starlings
gathered singing in the square –
like a shower of arrows they cross
the flash of a western window,
they bead the wires with jet,
they nestle preening by the lamps
and shine, sidling by the lamps
and sing, shining, they stir
the homeward hurrying crowds.
A man looks up and points
smiling to his son beside him
wide-eyed at the clamour on those cliffs –

it sinks, shrills out in waves,
levels to a happy murmur,
scatters in swooping arcs,
a stab of confused sweetness
that pierces the boy like a story,
a story more than a song.
He will never forget that evening,
the silhouette of the roofs,
the starlings by the lamps.

II

The City Chambers are hopping mad.
Councillors with rubber plugs in their ears!
Secretaries closing windows!
Window-cleaners want protection and danger money.
The Lord Provost can't hear herself think, man.
What's that?
Lord Provost, can't hear herself think.

At the General Post Office
the clerks write Three Pounds Starling in the savings-
    books.
Each telephone-booth is like an aviary.
I tried to send a parcel to County Kerry but –
The cables to Cairo got fankled, sir.
What's that?
I said the cables to Cairo got fankled.

And as for the City Information Bureau –
I'm sorry I can't quite chirrup did you twit –
No I wanted to twee but perhaps you can't cheep –
Would you try once again, that's better, I – sweet –
When's the last boat to Milngavie? Tweet?
What's that?
I said when's the last boat to Milngavie?

III

There is nothing for it now but scaffolding:
clamp it together, send for the bird-men,
Scarecrow Strip for the window-ledge landings,
Cameron's Repellent on the overhead wires.
Armour our pediments against eavesdroppers.
This is a human outpost. Save our statues.
Send back the jungle. And think of the joke:
as it says in the papers, it is very comical
to watch them alight on the plastic rollers
and take a tumble. So it doesn't kill them?
All right, so who's complaining? This isn't Peking
where they shoot the sparrows for hygiene and cash.
So we're all humanitarians, locked in our cliff-dwellings
encased in our repellent, guano-free and guilt-free.
The Lord Provost sings in her marble hacienda.
The Postmaster-General licks an audible stamp.
Sir Walter is vexed that his column's deserted.
I wonder if we really deserve starlings?
There is something to be said for these joyous messengers
that we repel in our indignant orderliness.
They lift up the eyes, they lighten the heart,
and some day we'll decipher that sweet frenzied whistling
as they wheel and settle along our hard roofs
and take those grey buttresses for home.
One thing we know they say, after their fashion.
They like the warm cliffs of man.

THE FIRST MEN ON MERCURY

— We come in peace from the third planet.
Would you take us to your leader?

— Bawr stretter! Bawr. Bawr. Stretterhawl?

– This is a little plastic model
of the solar system, with working parts.
You are here and we are there and we
are now here with you, is this clear?

– Gawl horrop. Bawr. Abawrhannahanna!

– Where we come from is blue and white
with brown, you see we call the brown
here 'land', the blue is 'sea', and the white
is 'clouds' over land and sea, we live
on the surface of the brown land,
all round is sea and clouds. We are 'men'.
Men come –

– Glawp men! Gawrbenner menko. Menhawl?

– Men come in peace from the third planet
which we call 'earth'. We are earthmen.
Take us earthmen to your leader.

– Thmen? Thmen? Bawr. Bawrhossop.
Yuleeda tan hanna. Harrabost yuleeda.

– I am the yuleeda. You see my hands,
we carry no benner, we come in peace.
The spaceways are all stretterhawn.

– Glawn peacemen all horrabhanna tantko!
Tan come at'mstrossop. Glawp yuleeda!

– Atoms are peacegawl in our harraban.
Menbat worrabost from tan hannahanna.

— You men we know bawrhossoptant. Bawr.
We know yuleeda. Go strawg backspetter quick.

— We cantantabawr, tantingko backspetter now!

— Banghapper now! Yes, third planet back.
Yuleeda will go back blue, white, brown
nowhanna! There is no more talk.

— Gawl han fasthapper?

— No. You must go back to your planet.
Go back in peace, take what you have gained
but quickly.

— Stretterworra gawl, gawl . . .

— Of course, but nothing is ever the same,
now is it? You'll remember Mercury.

GLASGOW SONNET

A mean wind wanders through the backcourt trash.
Hackles on puddles rise, old mattresses
puff briefly and subside. Play-fortresses
of brick and bric-a-brac spill out some ash.
Four storeys have no windows left to smash,
but in the fifth a chipped sill buttresses
mother and daughter the last mistresses
of that black block condemned to stand, not crash.
Around them the cracks deepen, the rats crawl.
The kettle whimpers on a crazy hob.

Roses of mould grow from ceiling to wall.
The man lies late since he has lost his job,
smokes on one elbow, letting his coughs fall
thinly into an air too poor to rob.

PILATE AT FORTINGALL

A Latin harsh with Aramaicisms
poured from his lips incessantly; it made
no sense, for surely he was mad. The glade
of birches shamed his rags, in paroxysms
he stumbled, toga'd, furred, blear, brittle, grey.
They told us he sat there beneath the yew
even in downpours; ate dog-scraps. Crows flew
from prehistoric stone to stone all day.
'See him now'. He crawled to the cattle-trough
at dusk, jumbled the water till it sloshed
and spilled into the hoof-mush in blue strands,
slapped with useless despair each sodden cuff,
and washed his hands, and watched his hands, and washed
his hands, and watched his hands, and washed his hands.

GLASGOW OCTOBER 1971

In an old Gallowgate cemetery
a woman kneeling at her mother's grave
has half risen to her feet, her arms
splayed forward and chrysanthemums
scattering from the vase she tramps on.
Her mouth is rounded out to scream
but the stab in her back is not deep —
no more than a memento mori
from the youth who sharpens his knife
nonchalant on the tombstone.

ALEXANDER SCOTT

CORONACH

For the deid o the 5th/7th Battalion, The Gordon Highlanders

Waement the deid
I never did,
Owre gled I was ane o the lave
That somewey baid alive
To trauchle my thowless hert
Wi ithers' hurt.

But nou that I'm far
Frae the fechtin's fear,
Nou I hae won awa frae aa thon pain
Back til my beuks and my pen,
They croud aroun me out o the grave
Whaur love and langourie sae lanesome grieve.

Cryan the cauld words:
'We hae dree'd our weirds,
But you that byde ahin,
Ayont our awesome hyne,
You are the flesh we aince had been,
We that are bruckle brokken bane.'

Cryan a drumlie speak:
'You hae the words we spak,
You hae the sang
We canna sing,
Sen death maun skail
The makar's skill.

'Makar, frae nou ye maun
Be singan for us deid men,
Sing til the warld we loo'd
(For aa that its brichtness lee'd)
And tell hou the sudden nicht
Cam doun and made us nocht.'

Waement the deid
I never did,
But nou I am safe awa
I hear their wae
Greetan greetan dark and daw,
Their death the-streen my darg the-day.

coronach, lament; *waement*, lament; *lave*, remainder; *baid*, stayed; *trauchle*,
trouble; *thowless*, spiritless; *fechtin*, fighting; *beuks*, books; *langourie*, longing;
dree'd, endured; *weirds*, fates; *byde*, remain; *ahin*, behind; *ayont*, beyond; *hyne*,
haven; *aince*, once; *bruckle*, brittle; *drumlie*, dull; *speak*, speech; *skail*, disperse;
makar, poet; *maun*, must; *loo'd*, loved; *lee'd*, lied; *nocht*, nothing; *greetan*,
weeping; *the-streen*, yesterday; *darg*, work; *the-day*, to-day.

HAAR IN PRINCES STREET

The heicht o the biggins is happit in rauchens o haar,
    The statues alane
    Stand clearly, heid til fit in stane,
And lour frae *then* and *thonder* at *hencefurth* and *here*.

The past on pedestals, girnan frae ilka feature,
      Wi granite frouns
    They glower at the present's feckless loons,
Its gangrels tint i the haar that fankles the future.

The fowk o flesh, stravaigan wha kens whither,
      And come frae whar,
    Hudder like ghaists i the gastrous haar,
Forfochten and wae i the smochteran smore o the weather.

They swaiver and flirn i the freeth like straes i the sea,
    An airtless swither,
    Steeran awa the t'ane frae t'ither,
Alane, and lawlie aye to be lanesome sae.

But heich i' the lift (whar the haar is skailan fairlie
    In blufferts o wind)
    And blacker nor nicht whan starns are blind,
The Castle looms — a fell, a fabulous ferlie.

Dragonish, darksome, dourly grapplan the Rock
    Wi claws o stane
    That scart our history bare til the bane,
It braks like Fate throu Time's wanchancy reek.

heicht, height; *biggins*, buildings; *happit*, covered; *rauchens*, mantles; *haar*, mist; *heid til fit*, head to foot; *thonder*, yonder; *girnan*, grimacing; *ilka*, every; *frouns*, frowns; *feckless*, incapable; *loons*, boys; *gangrels*, tramps, wanderers; *tint*, lost; *fankles*, entangles; *fowk*, folk; *stravaigan*, wandering; *whar*, where; *hudder*, huddle; *ghaists*, ghosts; *gastrous*, monstrous; *forfochten*, tired out; *wae*, sad; *smochteran*, smothering; *smore*, suffocation; *swaiver*, totter; *flirn*, twist; *freeth*, foam; *straes*, straws; *airtless*, without direction; *t'ane frae t'ither*, the one from the other; *lawlie*, loath; *lanesome*, lonely; *sae*, so; *lift*, sky; *skailan*, dispersing; *fairlie*, in good measure; *blufferts*, gusts; *nicht*, night; *starns*, stars; *fell*, terrible; *ferlie*, wonder; *dourly*, stubbornly; *scart*, scratch; *bane*, bone; *braks*, breaks; *wanchancy*, evil boding; *reek*, smoke.

PARADISE TINT

Said Adam til Eve,
'Ye've gart me grieve.'
Said Eve til Adam,
'Aipples, I've had 'em!'

Said Adam til Nick,
'Ye snake! Ye swick!'
Said Nick til Adam,
'Me — or the madam?'

Said Adam til 's sel,
'A wumman 's hell.'
Said 's sel til Adam,
'Doubled, ye'd wad 'em.'

Said Adam til God,
'What wey sae odd?'
Said God til Adam,
'Never ye'll faddom.'

gart, made; *swick*, cheat; *'s sel*, himself; *wad*, wed; *faddom*, fathom.

SABBATH
Come unto me, all ye that are heavy laden

The portly paunches trundled
the few short steps (O merciful religion!)
from the car to the door of the kirk,
the loaded furs lurching
from limousines to cushioned pews —

Pagan , I paused,
the Sunday papers under my infidel arm,
amazed at the joyful vision of
gentle Jesus
kicking camel-fat backsides
through a needle's eye.

From SCOTCHED

Scotch God
Kent His
Faither.

Scotch Religion
Damn
Aa.

Scotch Optimism
Through a gless,
Darkly.

Scotch Pessimism
Nae
Gless.

Scotch Drink
Nip
Trip.

Scotch Love
Barely
A bargain.

Scotch Free-love
Canna be
Worth much.

Scotch Lovebirds
Cheap
Cheep.

Scotch Passion
Forgot
Mysel.

Scotch Education
I tellt ye
I tellt ye.

PROBLEMS

('We have a problem here.' *Apollo 13's* report on an oxygen-tank failure)

The haill warld waited,
ten hunder million herts
in as monie mouths,
the haill warld harkened
til quaet voices
briggan the black howes o space

wi licht hope
o shipwrack saved,
the mune's mariners
steered through the stark lift
on a lifeline o skeelie science
(the wyve o human harns,
a hunder thousand hankan thegither
owre aa the waft o the warld)
that haled them frae toom heaven
to hame i the sea's haven
– and aye wi the camera's ee
the michty millions watched.

Ahint our backs,
the brukken corps o coolies
cam sooman alang the sworl
o the mirk Mekong,
their wyve o human harns
warped by the skeelie science
that made the machinegun's mant
the proof o pouer
to connach lifelines.

We hae a problem here.

briggan, bridging; *howes*, hollows; *stark lift*, bare sky; *skeelie*, skilful; *wyve*, weave; *harns*, brains; *hankan*, working like weavers; *thegither*, together; *waft*, weft; *toom*, empty; *brukken corps*, broken bodies; *sooman*, swimming; *mirk*, dark; *mant*, stammer; *connach*, destroy.

EXPLODING UNIVERSE

It aa began wi a bang,
a great muckle bang
that skited its stour til the hynest space
in a hotchan hotter o starns.

The haill hypothec,
aa the galactic glories,
began wi the ae colossal clapper,
a crack o sklenteran stew
that bairned the brankie suns.

Or sae they scrieve o't,
boffin billies,
eident on origins,
skeelie to speir at dernit atoms
and skinklan midnicht lifts
for 'the fact o the maitter',
the maitter o fact,
the maitter
that made us aa frae a muckle blatteran bang.

But wha was it lichted thon farawa fuse
and blew himsel to bleezes?

great muckle, mighty; *skited*, shot off; *stour*, dust; *hynest*, furthest; *hotchan*, swarming; *hotter*, simmer; *starns*, stars; *haill hypothec*, whole concern; *ae*, one; *clapper*, rattle; *crack*, moment; *sklenteran*, splintering; *stew*, dust; *bairned*, gave birth to; *brankie*, gaudy; *scrieve*, write; *billies*, fellows; *eident*, keen; *skeelie*, skilful; *speir*, enquire; *dernit*, secret; *skinklan*, sparkling; *lifts*, skies; *blatteran*, driving forcefully; *bleezes*, blazes.

DERICK THOMSON

CLANN-NIGHEAN AN SGADAIN

An gàire mar chraiteachan salainn
ga fhroiseadh bho 'm bial,
an sàl 's am picil air an teanga,
's na miaran cruinne, goirid a dheanadh giullachd,

no a thogadh leanabh gu socair, cuimir,
seasgair, fallain,
gun mhearachd,
's na sùilean cho domhainn ri fèath.

B'e bun-os-cionn na h-eachdraidh a dh' fhàg iad
'nan tràillean aig ciùrairean cutach,
thall 's a-bhos air Galldachd ' s an Sasuinn.
Bu shaillte an duais a thàrr iad
ás na mìltean bharaillean ud,
gaoth na mara geur air an craiceann,
is eallach a' bhochdainn 'nan ciste,
is mara b'e an gàire
shaoileadh tu gu robh an teud briste.

Ach bha craiteachan uaille air an cridhe,
ga chumail fallain,
is bheireadh cutag an teanga
slisinn á fanaid nan Gall –
agus bha obair rompa fhathast
nuair gheibheadh iad dhachaidh,
ged nach biodh maoin ac':
air oidhche robach gheamhraidh,
ma bha sud an dàn dhaibh,
dheanadh iad daoine.

THE HERRING GIRLS

Their laughter like a sprinkling of salt showered from their lips, brine and pickle on their tongues, and the stubby short fingers that could handle fish, or lift a child gently, neatly, safely, wholesomely, unerringly, and the eyes that were as deep as a calm.

The topsy-turvy of history had made them slaves to short-arsed curers, here and there in the Lowlands, in England. Salt the reward they won from those thousands of barrels, the sea-wind sharp on their skins, and the burden of poverty in their kists, and were it not for their laughter you might think the harp-string was broken.

But there was a sprinkling of pride on their hearts, keeping them sound, and their tongues' gutting-knife would tear a strip from the Lowlanders' mockery – and there was work awaiting them when they got home, though they had no wealth: on a wild winter's night, if that were their lot, they would make men.

CRUAIDH?

Cuil-lodair, is Briseadh na h-Eaglaise,
is briseadh nan tacannan –
lamhachas-làidir dà thriane de ar comas;
'se seòltachd tha dhìth oirnn.
Nuair s theirgeas a' chruaidh air faobhar na speala
caith bhuat a' chlach-lìomhaidh;
chan eil agad ach iarunnn bog
mur eil de churas 'nad innleachd na so sgathadh,

Is caith bhuat briathran mìne
oir chan fhada bhios briathran agad;
tha Tuatha Dé Danann fo'n talamh,
tha Tìr nan Og anns an Fhraing,
's nuair a ruigeas tu Tìr a' Gheallaidh,
mura bi thu air t' aire,
coinnichidh Sasunnach riut is plìon air,
a dh' innse dhut gun tug Dia, bràthair athar, còir dha anns an
    fhearann.

STEEL?

Culloden, the Disruption, and the breaking up of the tack-farms – two-thirds of our power is violence; it is cunning we need. When the tempered steel near the edge of the scythe-blade is worn, throw away the whetstone; you have nothing left but soft iron unless your intellect has a steel edge that will cut clean.

And throw away soft words, for soon you will have no words left; the Fathers of the Faery are underground, the Country of the Ever-Young is in France, and when you reach the Promised Land, unless you are on your toes, a bland Englishman will meet you, and say to you that God, his uncle, has given him a title to the land.

CISTEACHAN-LAIGHE

Duin' àrd, tana
's fiasag bheag air,
's locair 'na làimh:
gach uair theid mi seachad
air bùth-shaoirsneachd sa' bhaile,
's a thig gu mo chuimhne fàileadh na min-sàibh,
thig gu mo chuimhne cuimhne an àit ud,
le na cisteachan-laighe,
na h-ùird 's na tairgean,
na sàibh 's na sgeilbean,
is mo sheanair crom,
is sliseag bho shliseag ga locradh
bho'n bhòrd thana lom.

Mus robh fhios agam dé bh' ann bàs;
beachd, bloigh fios, boillsgeadh
de'n dorchadas, fathann de'n t-sàmchair.
'S nuair a sheas mi aig uaigh,
là fuar Earraich, cha dainig smuain
thugam air na cisteachan-laighe
a rinn esan do chàch:
'sann a bha mi 'g iarraidh dhachaidh,
far am biodh còmhradh, is tea, is blàths.

Is anns an sgoil eile cuideachd,
san robh saoir na h-inntinn a' locradh,
cha tug mi 'n aire do na cisteachan-laighe,
ged a bha iad 'nan suidhe mun cuairt orm;
cha do dh' aithnich mi 'm bréid Buerla,
an lìomh Gallda bha dol air an fhiodh,
cha do leugh mi na facail air a' phràis,
cha do thuig mi gu robh mo chinneadh a' dol bàs.

Gus an dainig gaoth fhuar an Earraich-sa
a locradh a' chridhe;
gus na dh' fhairich mi na tairgean a' dol tromham,
's cha shlànaich tea no còmhradh an cràdh.

COFFINS

A tall thin man with a short beard, and a plane in his hand: whenever I pass a joiner's shop in the city, and the scent of sawdust comes to my mind, memories return of that place, with the coffins, the hammers and nails, saws and chisels, and my grandfather, bent, planing shavings from a thin, bare plank.

Before I knew what death was; or had any notion, a glimmering of the darkness, a whispering of the stillness. And when I stood at his grave, on a cold Spring day, not a thought came to me of the coffins he made for others: I merely wanted home where there would be talk, and tea, and warmth.

And in the other school also, where the joiners of the mind were planing, I never noticed the coffins, though they were sitting all round me; I did not recognise the English braid, the Lowland varnish being applied to the wood, I did not read the words on the brass, I did not understand that my race was dying.

Until the cold wind of this Spring came to plane the heart; until I felt the nails piercing me, and neither tea nor talk will heal the pain.

LEODHAS AS T-SAMHRADH

An iarmailt cho soilleir tana
mar gum biodh am brat-sgàile air a reubadh
's an Cruthaidhear 'na shuidhe am fianuis a shluaigh
aig a' bhuntàt 's a sgadan,
gun duine ris an dean E altachadh.
'S iongantach gu bheil iarmailt air an t-saoghal
tha cur cho beag a bhacadh air daoine
sealltainn a-steach dha'n an t-sìorruidheachd;
chan eil feum air feallsanachd
far an dean thu chùis le do phrosbaig.

LEWIS IN SUMMER

The atmosphere clear and transparent as though the veil had been rent and the Creator were sitting in full view of His people eating potatoes and herring, with no man to whom He can say grace. Probably there's no other sky in the world that makes it so easy for people to look in on eternity; you don't need philosophy where you can make do with binoculars.

SIANSADH AN DEALACHAIDH

Solas bho sholas a' dol às
is ceòl nan teud a' falbh 's a' tighinn,
bogha ga phasgadh
is còrn ga thogail
's an ceòl fann a' tighinn 's a' falbh,
taibhsean aig cùl na stèids;
binn, binn ceòl an eadar-sholais,
an t-eadar-sholas a' toirt a-mach a' bhinn,
's an stèids a' cur cùl ri beatha;
an teud a' fàs fann,
an dorchadas a' fàs,
an còrn ga fhosgladh 's ga phasgadh,
an t-saighead ga toirt às a' bhogha;
an ceòl a' dol anns a' brugh;
oidhche smàlaidh nan coinneal a' dol seachad.

FAREWELL SYMPHONY

(Hamburg, 28/3/82, after a performance of Haydn's Abschiedssinfonie)

The lights go out one by one and the string music comes and goes, a bow is lowered, a horn raised, the soft music rises and falls, ghosts at the back of the stage; sweet, sweet the twilight music, twilight delivers its sweet sentence, and the stage turns its back on life; the string grows frail, the darkness grows, the horn is taken out and put away, the arrow removed from the bow; the music goes into the fairy mound; the night of snuffed-out candles passes.

GEORGE MACKAY BROWN

WEDDING

With a great working of elbows
The fiddlers ranted
—Joy to Ingrid and Magnus!

With much boasting and burning
The whisky circled
　　—Wealth to Ingrid and Magnus!

With deep clearings of the throat
The minister intoned
'Thirdly, Ingrid and Magnus' . . .

Ingrid and Magnus stared together
When midnight struck
At a white unbroken bed.

THE OLD WOMEN

Go sad or sweet or riotous with beer
Past the old women gossiping by the hour,
They'll fix on you from every close and pier
An acid look to make your veins run sour.

'No help,' they say, 'his grandfather that's dead
Was troubled with the same dry-throated curse,
And many a night he made the ditch his bed.
This blood comes welling from the same cracked source.'

On every kind of merriment they frown.
But I have known a gray-eyed sober boy
Sail to the lobsters in a storm, and drown.
Over his body dripping on the stones
Those same old hags would weave into their moans
An undersong of terrible holy joy.

THE FINISHED HOUSE

In the finished house, a flame is brought to the hearth.
Then a table, between door and window
Where a stranger will eat before the men of the house.
A bed is laid in a secret corner
For the three agonies—love, birth, death—
That are made beautiful with ceremony.
The neighbours come with gifts—
A set of cups, a calendar, some chairs.
A fiddle is hung at the wall.
A girl puts lucky salt in a dish.
The cupboard has its loaf and bottle.
On the seventh morning
One spills water of blessing over the threshold.

DEAD FIRES

At Burnmouth the door hangs from a broken hinge
And the fire is out.

The windows of Shore empty sockets
And the hearth coldness.

At Bunertoon the small drains are choked.
Thrushes sing in the chimney.

Stars shine through the roofbeams of Scar.
No flame is needed
To warm ghost and nettle and rat.

Greenhill is sunk in a new bog.
No kneeling woman
Blows red wind through squares of ancient turf.

The Moss is a tumble of stones.
That one black stone
Is the stone where the hearth fire was rooted.

In Crawnest the sunken hearth
Was an altar for priests of legend,
Old seamen from the clippers with silken beards.

The three-toed pot at the wall of Park
Is lost to woman's cunning.
A slow fire of rust eats the cold iron.

The sheep drift through Reumin all winter.
Sheep and snow
Blanch fleetingly the black stone.

From that sacred stone the children of the valley
Drifted lovewards
And out of labour to the lettered kirkyard stone.

The fire beat like a heart in each house
From the first cornerstone
Till they led through a sagging lintel the last old one.

The poor and the good fires are all quenched.
Now, cold angel, keep the valley
From the bedlam and cinders of A Black Pentecost.

HADDOCK FISHERMEN

Midnight. The wind yawing nor-east.
A low blunt moon.
Unquiet beside quiet wives we rest.

A spit of rain and a gull
In the open door.
The lit fire. A quick mouthful of ale.

We push the *Merle* at a sea of cold flame.
The oars drip honey.
Hook by hook uncoils under The Kame.

Our line breaks the trek of sudden thousands.
Twelve nobbled jaws,
Gray cowls, gape in our hands,

Twelve cold mouths scream without sound.
The sea is empty again.
Like tinkers the bright ones endlessly shift their ground.

We probe emptiness all the afternoon,
Then pause and fill our teeth
With dependable food, beef and a barley scone.

Sunset drags its butcher blade
From the day's throat.
We turn through an ebb salt and sticky as blood.

More stars than fish. Women, cats, a gull
Mewl at the rock.
The valley divides the meagre miracle.

KIRKYARD

A silent conquering army,
The island dead,
Column on column, each with a stone banner
Raised over his head.

A green wave full of fish
Drifted far
In wavering westering ebb-drawn shoals beyond
Sinker or star.

A labyrinth of celled
And waxen pain.
Yet I come to the honeycomb often, to sip the finished
Fragrance of men.

KEN MORRICE

CAUL KAIL

Rigs stan erect, great iron teats
    on the breist o the sea.
We sook the black milk up and up
    until the wall gangs dry.

And gin the ile's aa teem and deen,
    the bonny fish aa catchit,
fit then? Tartan tourist whigmaleeries?
    Trips roun the roosty ile-rigs?

'Gweed maisters,' we'll hae tae parleyvoo
in their ain leid
tae Eytalians, Frenchies, and stoot German lairdies,
daffin oor bonnets,

'Welcome tae Caledonia! The ile, maisters,
finally got on oor wick.
But tak a gless ev'noo tae wash doon
yer authentic neep brose.'

Syne we'll fa tee tae keep the toon,
set oot new kailyairds.
A grippy nation like oors canna but learn
tae pit its mou tae the bottle.

Or, gin its teem, sook its ain thoomb.

sook, suck; *wall*, well; *ile*, oil; *teem*, empty; *deen*, done; *fit*, what; *whigmaleeries*,
useless ornaments; *gweed*, good; *leid*, language; *ev'noo*, just now; *neep*, turnip; *fa tee*,
fall to; *kailyards*, cabbage-patches; *grippy*, miserly

OLD PHOTOGRAPH: FISHERMAN AND WIFE

These salt-hard hands gave few caresses.

Acts of love in those days
meant just another mouth to feed.
Yet heart and lips were soft enough,
bed no narrower than need.

Weary of wind and sea,
of partings and the lonely shore,
of danger looming and drudgery's defeats,
yet the two of them seem more
at one than we do, thigh-to-thigh,
liberated on our king-size sheets.

Bound and stiff in bible-black,
matched, together, the halves are one,
whole and loving in their lack.

ALASTAIR MACKIE

IN ABSENTIA

'We've no heard frae God this while,'
said ane o the angels.
It was at a synod.
o the metaphors.

Cam a wind;
it was a aabody speirin
'Wha?'
intill themsels.

It was heard by the sauls
o Baudelaire and Pascal.
They fell thro the muckle hole
opened by the question.

I the boddom Jesus sweatit
'Consummatum est.'
And Nietzsche
hou he laucht and laucht.

The maist o fowk bein neither
philosophers or theologians
kept gaun tae the kirk.
Whiles, like.

Syne God said: 'Noo I'm awa,
mak a kirk or a mill o't.'

And God gaed tae the back o beyond
i the midst o aathing.

speirin, asking; *laucht,* laughed; *whiles,* sometimes

ADOLESCENCE

Gin they wad leave me alane!

Whit ails me
I dinna ken.

Look ahint my een, ye'll fin
het saut and grienin.

Thae days it cams easy
like—dinna greet lassie—

A beast mum and tethert
tae a stound.

The soond o the guitars
and me dwaumin thro them.

And did he no smile tae me?
But he did smile tae me!

The keekin-gless is my frien
I tell it aathing jist lookin.

It says naething the haill time
but—Ye're bonny quine—

I fill up its laneliness
wi my ain dowie face

and when my een crack
it shares my hert-brak

cut gless lookin at cut gless.

het saut, hot salt; *grienin,* yearning; *greet,* weep; *stound,* pang; *dwaumin,* dreaming;
quine, girl; *dowie,* sad

HAND

It's a delta o functions,
aeons hae soopled.

And a map
runkled wi high roads.

A cleuk forby
I share wi the beasts.

And a barescrape
wi a skiftin o strae hair.

It has the face's weather,
its stretch o moods;

it can straik love
and thraw thrapples;

or be lowsed
in dreichness or soon sleep.

Its finger-nebs
snuff the skin o the world—

flooers, stane, wid, metal,
the things, oor neebors.

Brigs it maks
oot o handshaks.

Blinner than the een
it fichers in the dark

for the airt o things,
door-sneck or shouther-bane.

When the condies o the body
stop their pumpin

the hands lie on the breist
cuddling their tool bags.

soopled, made supple; runkled, wrinkled; cleuk, claw; skiftin, touch; strae, straw; straik, stroke; thraw thrapples, twist throats; lowsed, loosed; dreichness, dullness; nebs, noses; wid, wood; brigs, bridges; blinner, blinder; fichers, fumbles; airt, direction; sneck, latch; shouther-bane, shoulder-bone; condies, drains

IAIN CRICHTON SMITH

OLD WOMAN

And she, being old, fed from a mashed plate
as an old mare might droop across a fence
to the dull pastures of its ignorance.
Her husband held her upright while he prayed

to God who is all-forgiving to send down
some angel somewhere who might land perhaps
in his foreign wings among the gradual crops.
She munched, half dead, blindly searching the spoon.

Outside, the grass was raging. There I sat
imprisoned in my pity and my shame
that men and women having suffered time
should sit in such a place, in such a state

and wished to be away, yes, to be far away
with athletes, heroes, Greeks or Roman men
who pushed their bitter spears into a vein
and would not spend an hour with such decay.

'Pray God,' he said, 'we ask you, God,' he said.
The bowed back was quiet. I saw the teeth
tighten their grip around a delicate death.
And nothing moved within the knotted head

but only a few poor veins as one might see
vague wishless seaweed floating on a tide
of all the salty waters where had died
too many waves to mark two more or three.

TWO GIRLS SINGING

It neither was the words nor yet the tune.
Any tune would have done and any words.
Any listener or no listener at all.

As nightingales in rocks or a child crooning
in its own world of strange awakening
or larks for no reason but themselves.

So on the bus through late November running
by yellow lights tormented, darkness falling,
the two girls sang for miles and miles together

and it wasn't the words or tune. It was the singing.
It was the human sweetness in that yellow,
the unpredicted voices of our kind.

SUNDAY MORNING WALK

Sunday of wrangling bells—and salt in the air—
I passed the tall black men and their women walking
over the tight-locked streets which were all on fire
with summer ascendant. The seas were talking and talking

as I took my way to the wood where the river ran quiet.
The grass lay windowed in sunlight, the leaves were raging
in furious dying green. The road turned right
round the upstanding castle whose stone, unaging

marks how a world remains as I, being now
pack of wandering flesh, take holiday, strolling
far from the churches' declaiming. Health will allow
riots of naiads and nymphs, so wantonly rolling

with me in leaves in woods, thinking how once
Jove took his pleasure of Leda or—splendid embracing—
god would mate with a goddess—rapid the pounce,
fruitful the hot-thighed meeting, no need for unlacing.

And occupied thus, I came where a dead sheep lay
close to a fence, days gone. The flies were hissing and buzzing
out of the boiling eyes, wide open as day.
I stood in the sunlight beside it, watching and musing.

Three crows famished yards off. Live sheep grazed far
from the rotting carcass. The jaw, well-shaved, lay slackly
there on the warm quiet grass. The household air
was busy with buzzing like fever. How quickly, how quickly

the wool was peeled from the back! How still was the flesh!
How the visiting flies would knock at the door of the sockets!
How the hole in the side gaped red, a well-sized gash!
How the clear young lambs grazed in the shade of the
      thickets!

And the sun blazed on my shoulder. Here was no shade
but the sheep was quiet, so quiet. There was nothing to notice
but the grape-bunched flies and the crows. Could a world
      have stayed
if I'd taken a stick in my hand to beat off the flies?

They would merely return when I'd gone and busy as always
inhabit this larder again no matter how brightly
I struck with my smart sharp stick. All I could praise—
yes, all I could praise—was the sheep lying there so quietly

not knowing, not knowing. High summer was raging around.
I stood in my slack clean clothes. The stones were burning.
The flies in the wound continued their occupied sound
as I turned my back on a death of no weeping or mourning.

AT THE FIRTH OF LORNE

In the cold orange light we stared across
to Mull and Kerrera and far Tiree.
A setting sun emblazoned your bright knee
to a brilliant gold to match your hair's gold poise.

Nothing had changed: the world was as it was
a million years ago. The slaty stone
slept in its tinged and aboriginal iron.
The sky might flower a little, and the grass

perpetuate its sheep. But from the sea
the bare bleak islands rose, beyond the few
uneasy witticisms we let pursue
their desolate silences. There was no tree

nor other witness to the looks we gave
each other there, inhuman as if tolled
by some huge bell of iron and of gold,
I no great Adam and you no bright Eve.

RETURN TO LEWIS (6)

Down on the sand the visitors turn brown.
Their children plunge in roaring waves that bring
the blue shells shoreward, and whose uttering
is not in Gaelic but an ignorant tongue
relentless and obscure no poet's sung
nor slant-capped peasant decent by his fence
rooted in time and grass and reticence,
while the sky curves from moor to treeless moor
and the only colour is his painted door.
The squealing children rush the waves and run
pursued by water towards the white sun
which broils their parents to a crablike hue.
I gaze intently into that large blue
astounding acreage imagining the seals,
blunt-headed sharks, and the gigantic whales,

in playful motion while here deep in grass
the cows munch endlessly and packed mini-cars
wait for the tourists whose sand-castles fade
into the ocean's blind monotonous trade.

THE VOICE

I hear in this valley which is loud with streams
a voice that cries, 'You are a guilty sinner,'
and this is what the desolate Highlands mean.
'Guilty, guilty,' that voice cries and cries
though the delicate deer don't hear it, and they don't raise
their heads out of the grass, and the sheep feed
steadily, contentedly. But the voice
grows louder and louder endlessly passing sentence
from the black mountain peaks that tower around
and saying in the noise of flowing waters,
'Guilty sinner, when will you ever see
the blackness of the stone, in the rhododendrons
the devilish snake uprising, in the sunset
the blood of the long-judged who burn with Me?'

IN THE CASTLE

A black marble clock is ticking
among the embroidery Queen Mary made
on some of the lonely nights before she died.
The thin greyish armour has been broken

by a hole in the middle where the heart might be.
In a painting on a wall a haughty girl
is smiling towards a pheasant which an earl,
thin as a lath, has shot. This I can see

is the world of the stupid bulging-eyed young lords,
foxes and horses. In a room of green
there's a painting of an eighteenth-century scene,
of ladies picknicking on a level sward,

and swords and snuff boxes, medals everywhere,
deer skulls and antlers, men in fiery kilts
standing in big frames of fading gilt,
servants behind them silent as old chairs,

claw-legged tables: letters from King Charles
to his good friend the laird to send some men
to stand up for their country and his reign,
and everywhere the bare-necked haughty girls.

Power to the stupid! Nature taken back
into the castle which the ignorant rule.
Keen-eyed Lloyd George riding a bicycle
as guest among the horses—on a rock

talking to a moustache as white as Haig's,
lips of a waterfall. The swords are withered
by the new machine-gun which destroys the heathered
landscape where they sit among silver plaques.

The stupid and courageous! 'Lord George killed . . .
is buried . . . Vimy Ridge.' And there he stares
downward on the tourist, trim and fierce,
dull eagle from a sky of polished gilt.

And the black clock ticks on among the French
and German accents. The black cameras whirr.
These are the great great grandchildren of the war
in which the lairds once served, scarred trench on trench,

horses on windy ridges, on a blue
morning of armour, leaf on leaf, great sword
held in the fading hand, when nothing stirred
but love of acres, horses, and the true

proud-necked and salmon-bodied supple lady
sitting in her room among her combs
coroneted, golden: and her home's
mahogany furniture seemingly so steady

while the black clock ticks on and from the trees
the pheasants are exploding towards the guns
and the seething servants once as still as stones
begin to climb slowly from bended knees.

WHEN DAY IS DONE

Sorrow remembers us when day is done.
It sits in its old chair gently rocking
and singing tenderly in the evening.
It welcomes us home again after the day.
It is so old in its black silken dress,
its stick beside it carved with legends.
It tells its stories over and over again.
After a while we have to stop listening.

NUAIR A BHIOS MI LEUGHADH

Nuair a bhios mi leughadh
litreachais mo dhaoine
bidh mi smaoineachadh,
'Chan eil Hòmair againn.

'No bàrd cho mór ri sin
idir cho mór ri sin
anns an dòigh sin
anns an dòigh mhiorbhaileach sin.'

Ach leughaidh mi 'n dràsda 's a rithist
mu dheidhinn nighean àraid
a tha bàsachadh leis a' ghaol
ann an dreasa ragach.

No éirigh iolair bho chloich
ag éigheachd, 'Bha mi 'g ithe
saighdearan uasal marbh
inan laighe air faiche.'

Is seòlaidh an dràsda 's rithist
air cuan a null a Chanada
soithichean le siùil shaillte,
òrain tha geal le pian.

WHEN I AM READING

When I am reading the literature of my people I am thinking, 'We haven't a Homer.

'Or any bard as great as that, at all as great as that, in that way, in that miraculous way.'

But I read now and again about a certain girl who is dying of love in a ragged dress.

Or an eagle will rise from a stone crying, 'I was eating a noble dead army lying on a field.'

And now and again there will sail on the sea over to Canada ships with salt sails, songs that are white with pain.

A' DOL DHACHAIDH

Am màireach théid mi dhachaidh do m'eilean
a' fiachainn ri saoghal a chur an diochuimhn'.
Togaidh mi dòrn de fhearann 'nam làmhan
no suidhidh mi air tulach inntinn
a' coimhead 'a' bhuachaill aig an spréidh.'

Dìridh (tha mi smaointinn) smeòrach.
Eiridh camhanaich no dhà.
Bidh bàt' 'na laighe ann an dcàrrsadh
na gréin iarail: 's bùrn a' ruith
troimh shaoghal shamhlaidhean mo thùir.

Ach bidh mi smaointinn (dh'aindeoin sin)
air an teine mhór th'air cùl ar smuain,
Nagasàki 's Hiroshima,
is cluinnidh mi ann an rùm leam fhìn
taibhs' no dhà a' sìor-ghluasad,

taibhs' gach mearachd, taibhs' gach cionta,
taibhs' gach uair a ghabh mi seachad
air fear leòint' air rathad clachach,
taibhs' an neonitheachd a' sgrùdadh
mo sheòmar balbh le aodann céin,

gu'm bi an t-eilean mar an àirc
'g éirigh 's a' laighe air cuan mór
's gun fhios an till an calman tuilleadh
's daoine a' bruidhinn 's a' bruidhinn ri chéile
's bogha-froise maitheanais 'nan deuran.

GOING HOME

Tomorrow I shall go home to my island trying to put a world into forgetfulness. I will lift a fistful of its earth in my hands or I will sit on a hillock of the mind watching 'the shepherd at his sheep.'

There will arise (I presume) a thrush. A dawn or two will break. There will be a boat lying in the glitter of the western sun: and water running through the world of similes of my intelligence.

But I will be thinking (in spite of that) of the great fire at the back of our thoughts, Nagasaki and Hiroshima, and I will hear in a room by myself a ghost or two ceaselessly moving,

the ghost of each error, the ghost of each guilt, the ghost of each time I walked past a wounded man on a stony road, the ghost of nothingness scrutinising my dumb room with distant face, till the island becomes an ark rising and falling on a great sea and I not knowing whether the dove will return and men talking and talking to each other and the rainbow of forgiveness in their tears.

DONALD MACAULAY

PRIOSAN

Chunnaic mi eun sèimh
sèimh an diugh air iteig,

chunnaic mi geal e
a mach air uinneig mo sheòmair,

chunnaic mi e saor
a' tighinn 's a' falbh troimh m' fhaicsinn;

's bha a shiubhal foirf'
air mheidh bil sgèith a' seòladh.

Lean an dealbh air mo sgàthan,
an cridhe dol mu'n cuairt gu mion air,

an inntinn ghionach
a' sealg air gus a thuigsinn,

's mi a' strì ri uinneag
fhosgladh
a' stri ri ruighinn air mo sheòlaid.

PRISON

I saw a smooth gentle bird today flying,

I saw it white out of the window of my room,

I saw it free flying in and out of my sight;

and its motion was flawless sailing on balanced wingtips.

The image stayed in my mirror, the heart encircling it minutely,

the greedy mind stalking it in order to understand it,

as I strove to get a window open, strove to make contact with my element.

COMHARRA STIUIRIDH

Siud an t-eilean ás an t-sealladh
mar a shiùbhlas am bàta,
mar a chunnaic iomadh bàrd e
eadar liunn is iargan,
's fir eile a bha 'n teanga fo fiscaill,
's deòir a' dalladh—
dùbradh neo-dhearbht is uinneagan a' fannadh.

Ach chan eil a' cheiste cho sìmplidh
do 'n allmharach an comhair na bliadhna:
a-mach á tilleadh éiridh iargan
á roinn a chuir an saoghal an dìmeas.

Cuideachd, chan e siud m' eilean-s':
chaidh esan fodha o chionn fhada,
a' chuid mhór dheth,
fo dheireas is ainneart;
's na chaidh fodha annam fhìn dheth,
'na ghrianan 's cnoc eighre,
tha e a' seòladh na mara anns am bì mi
'na phrìomh chomharr stiùridh
cunnartach, do-sheachaint, gun fhaochadh.

LANDMARK

There goes the island out of sight as the boat sails on, as seen by many a bard through sorrow and beer and by others, tongue under tooth, and tears blinding—an ill-defined shadow and windows fading.

But the matter is not so simple to the one who's a yearly pilgrim: out of returning sorrow rises from a region the world has derided.

And, that is not my island: it submerged long ago, the greater part of it, in neglect and tyranny—and the part that submerged in me of it, sun-bower and iceberg, sails the ocean I travel, a primary landmark dangerous, essential, demanding.

TOM BUCHAN

THE EVERLASTING ASTRONAUTS

These dead astronauts cannot decay—
they bounce on the quilted walls of their tin grave
and very gently collide with polythene balloons
full of used mouthwash, excrements and foodscraps.

They were chosen not for their imagination
but for their compatibility with machines—
glancing out at the vast America of the universe
they cried, 'Gee boys, it's great up here!'

Now, tumbling and yawning, their playpen hurries
into the continuum and at last they are real explorers
voyaging endlessly among unrecorded splendours
with Columbus, Peary, Magellan and Drake.

DUNCAN GLEN

MY FAITHER

Staunin nou aside his braw bress-haunled coffin
I mind him fine aside the black shinin range
In his grey strippit troosers, galluses and nae collar
For the flannel shirt. My faither.

I ken him fine thae twenty or mair years ago
Wi his great bauchles and flet auld kep;
And in his pouch the spottit reid neepkin
For usin wi snuff. My faither.

And ben in the lobby abune the braw shoon and spats
Aside the silk waistcoat and claw-haimmer jaicket
Wi its muckle oxter pouch, hung thc lum hat.
They caa'd him Jock the Lum. My faither.

And nou staunin wi thae braw shinin haunles
See him and me baith laid out in the best
Black suitin wi proper white aa weel chosen.
And dinna ken him. *My father.*

braw, fine; *bress-haunled,* brass-handled; *galluses,* braces; *hauchles,* old shoes; *flet auld kep,* flat old cap; *neepkin,* napkin; *shoon,* shoes; *claw-haimmer jaicket,* swallow-tail jacket; *oxter pouch,* armpit pocket; *lum hat,* top-hat

THE EDGE

Thae astronauts that sit and look at space
can they face the finite? Or tak the infinite?

Can they think o the edge o space and time
—and faa in? Naethin easier and nae steps
comin out. Is it like the grandest soomin pule
wi nae end to the deep end? Is it the end o the end?
Mebbe the air abune God's lap?

Or time itsel gaein back to the stert
at the end? Or the end at the stert?

Are you haly mystic? Spinnin a word wheel?
Astronaut got aff on the wrang orbit
and up against the infinite
—or the finite space? Are we
juist about to gae unner wi gas? In the
dentist's chair aa the time? Or me wi you?

Is this the inner warld? Ae eternity
—ayont the space and time we canna ken?

As we drap I lauch (wi God?)
Mebbe there's owre much oxygen
here ayont space and time. I launch and cry
I. I. I.
And landin claim aa for aa.

I face mysel.

faa, fall; *soomin pule,* swimming pool; *abune,* above; *ae,* one single; *ayont,* beyond

THE HERT O THE CITY

'In Glasgow, that damned sprawling evil town.' G. S. Fraser

I'm juist passin through
late at nicht. I risk a walk doun
through the gloomy tiled tunnel o Central Station
to Argyle Street and the Hielantman's Umbrella
for auld time's sake.
I see them at aince. Three girls and a wee fella
wi a bleedin heid. He's shakin wi laughter
and the bluid's splatterin on the shop windae.
I'm juist about awa back up the stairs when they're
aa round me. 'On your ain?' 'It's awfu cauld!'
'Ye shouldna be here by yersel!'

I canna help but notice the smell o drink and dirt.
His heid's a terrible sicht.

I look round but I *am* on my ain.
'Whaur are you from?' 'Preston?' 'You'll know Blackpool?'
Soon he'll hae my haill life story out o me.

'You maun be cauld' and
'Ye shouldna be here by yersel.'

I offer them some money to get in out o the càuld
but they laugh at the idea. They're no hungry
and there's plenty wine left.

They'll get fixed up themorrow.
It's warm enough unner the brig.

They'd walk me back safe to my pletform
but the polis 'll be in the station.

'Ye shouldna be here by yersel.'

STEWART CONN

TODD

My father's white uncle became
Arthritic and testamental in
Lyrical stages. He held cardinal sin
Was misuse of horses, then any game

Won on the sabbath. A Clydesdale
To him was not bells and sugar or declension
From paddock, but primal extension
Of rock and soil. Thundered nail

Turned to sacred bolt. And each night
In the stable he would slaver and slave
At cracked hooves, or else save
Bowls of porridge for just the right

Beast. I remember I lied
To him once, about oats: then I felt
The brand of his loving tongue, the belt
Of his own horsey breath. But he died,

When the mechanised tractor came to pass.
Now I think of him neighing to some saint
In a simple heaven or, beyond complaint,
Leaning across a fence and munching grass.

VISITING HOUR

In the pond of our new garden
were five orange stains, under
inches of ice. Weeks since anyone
had been there. Already by far
the most severe winter for years.
You broke the ice with a hammer.
I watched the goldfish appear,
blunt-nosed and delicately clear.

Since then so much has taken place
to distance us from what we were.
That it should come to this.
Unable to hide the horror
in my eyes, I stand helpless
by your bedside and can do no more
than wish it were simply a matter
of smashing the ice and giving you air.

AMBER

In an antique shop in the Lawnmarket
    Among lacquered trinketry and ivory
Figurines, are five amber apples
    The size of a half-fist: each a source
Of wonder, below its translucent surface.

The dealer who unearthed them must care
    As little for their future
As their past—letting them gather dust
    In this window, whose syrupy light
Spills across grey cobbles. Imagine them

Round the neck of a billowing contralto
    Or goitred senator's wife. If pearls drip,
These are a thunder-plump. Too gross
    For any ordinary voluptuary, they'd have graced
Clytemnestra there by the pillar, the axe bare;

Or been baubles fit for a temple cat:
    Having already survived from primordial
Gloom, sucked down and glacially compressed,
    Then washed to the shore. Today's pine forests
Await their turn, oozing globs of resin.

OF THIS TIME, IN THAT PLACE

Hard enough, those bronzed surf-riders from Bondi
At the next table, guzzling oysters and white wine,
To recall our summers, Uist's outline
A dismal blur, the division between sea and sky
Imperceptible, the dominant sound seepage of rain.

More difficult still to envisage, in the early
Years of last century, families brutally taken
Aboard ship, their crofts burned, given no option
But colonise 'the young country.'
Yet how tempting to bemoan those who are dead and gone,

When the wrongs to be righted are to-day's:
Among my memories, astonishing cockatoos
Screeching through gum-trees, koalas high on eucalyptus;
And everyone clamming up at my tactless
Questions about land-rights and the aborigines.

Now, Australian friends visiting our northern fastness,
The boot is on the other foot. I try to ease
My liberal conscience, pointing out how helpless
We are, over those issues that most concern us.
The yellow car-sticker curls . . . *Hands off Torness.*

STEPHEN MULRINE

THE COMING OF THE WEE MALKIES

Whit'll ye dae when the wee Malkies come,
if they dreep doon affy the wash-hoose dyke,
an pit the hems oan the sterrheid light,
an play keepie-up oan the clean close-wa',
an blooter yir windae in wi the baw,
missis, whit'll ye dae?

Whit'll ye dae when the wee Malkies come,
if they chap yir door, an choke yir drains,
an caw the feet fae yir sapsy weans,
an tummle thur wulkies through yir sheets,
an tim thur ashes oot in the street,
missis, whit'll ye dae?

Whit'll ye dae when the wee Malkies come,
if they chuck thur screwtaps doon the pan,
an stick thc hcid oan the sanit'ry man;
when ye hear thum shauchlin doon yir loaby,
chantin, 'Wee Malkies! The gemme's a bogey!'
—Haw, missis, whit'll ye dae?

dreep, drop; *pit the hems oan,* put out of action; *blooter,* smash; *tummle thur
wulkies,* turn cartwheels; *the gemme's a bogey,* the game's up

JAMES AITCHISON

LANDSCAPE WITH LAPWINGS

It's another April, and a day
with all the seasons in it, with lapwings
falling out of sunlight into rain,
stalling on a squall and then tumbling
over the collapsing wall of air
to float in zones of weightlessness again.

And on a day like this in such a place—
a few square miles of moorland in a round
of rounded hills, rain clouds and scattered trees,
with water flowing clearly over stone—
in such a place I feel the weights slip off
the way a lapwing would if it were me.

The place might form a frame of reference
for calculating weightlessness, and all
the weathers that are in one April day,
for drawing what conclusions can be drawn
from lapwings tumbling in and out of light
with such a total lack of gravity.

'DRUNK, OR STUNNED, OR DEAD?'

Drunk, or stunned, or dead? I couldn't say
that night beside the bus shelter. He lay
face downward on the pavement. As I rolled
him over on to his back a few coins spilled
slowly from his half-cupped hand. I saw
the big bruise on his forehead, bright and raw
against that hollow death-mask of a face.
An ambulance arrived, and then the police.
No one in the little crowd could tell
who he was, or how and when he fell.
Dead, or stunned, or drunk? I never found
out which it was. I heard the fading sound
of sirens in the night as I walked home,
and then an after-echo, the tinkling chime
of coins falling, spilling into the street
from his hand falling open at my feet.

DONALD CAMPBELL

JIST SHOWS YE!

Maist byordnar. Stotterin hame at five
o'clock on a sunny Sunday mornin
I kicked (accidental-like) a chip o stane
that wheeched
owre the waa o a neebor's gairden
landin (wi a daud!)
on the unsuspectin heid of a puir wee
blackie wha (mindin nae dout the auld saw)
was howkin maist eidently
for a fine fat creashy worm
in the dew-soakit, early-mornin sile.

The stane was haurd and shairp.
The blackie forbye hadnae ony kind o warnin.
He gied a 'kraak' and cloitit doun
flat on his back in a flaffer o pain
　　　(and aa for mindin nae mair nor a blackie's business
　　　—as I had been mindin my ain).

Aweel, thocht I, ae bad turn deserves a guid ane!
And, raxin owre, I cawed the cratur up
intil my breist, gently strokin
the flafferin wings, shushin and quaetenin
the squawk o his panic
wi the douce and daft-like noises
we humans mak at sicna times.

Syne, aa at aince, the flafferin stopped
the squawkin ceased
the hert pit an end til its thump-thump-thumpin.
The puir wee cratur died—and was at peace.

Dearie me.
I laid him doun and was jist in time
tae see the jammiest worm in Embro snoovin awa
intil the clairty refuge o the earth.

Jist shows ye!
And whiles ye cannae dae onythin richt . . .

maist byordnar, most extraordinary; *stotterin,* staggering; *wheeched,* whizzed;
blackie, blackbird; *mindin,* remembering; *howkin,* digging; *eidently,* eagerly;
creashy, greasy; *sile,* soil; *forbye,* besides; *cloitit,* fell heavily; *flaffer,* flutter; *raxin
owre,* reaching over; *cawed,* moved; *cratur,* creature; *douce,* gentle; *sicna,* such;
syne, then; *aa at aince,* all at once; *jammiest,* luckiest; *snoovin,* gliding; *clairty,*
dirty; *whiles,* sometimes

THE WINDS O JANUARY

Just as if they kent
just as if they'd heard frae history
the winds o January
blaw boisterous and bauld
owre aa creation, owre aa our warld.

It's a time
for cleanin out and reddin up.
The winds come
to clear the debris and teem awa
the aff-casts o progress. They sough
and strain and scour and strip richt doun
aa that reality requires. They move
as shairly as day follows nicht. They tyauve
and hunt as siccarly
as a vacuum vanquishes stour.

We lie in our beds and wonder.

Ahint the blin waas o our clenched minds
our thochts fecht and squabble wi the panic
o brattlin rats. Unsleepin and withouten speech
we hear the teeth o thon gale
ruggin at our rattlin rooves, our aiken doors.
Ticht in the dark, we fear the force
the sichtless scrannin at our safety
our weill-steekit winnock panes.
We lie in the daurk and wonder, wonder, wonder . . .

The auld year has tellt us nocht.
It never daes.

kent, knew; *bauld,* bold; *reddin,* tidying; *teem,* empty; *sough,* sigh; *shairly,* surely;
tyauve, work hard; *siccarly,* certainly; *stour,* dust; *ahint,* behind; *brattlin,*
squabbling; *ruggin,* tugging; *aiken,* oak; *scrannin,* scraping; *weill-steekit,* well-shut

DOUGLAS DUNN

THE HARP OF RENFREWSHIRE

Contemplating a map

Annals of the trilled R, gently stroked L,
Lamenting O of local literature,
Open, on this, their one-page book, a still
Land-language chattered in a river's burr.

Small-talk of herdsmen, rural argument—
These soft disputes drift over river-meadows,
A darg of conversations, a verbal scent—
Tut-tutted discourse, time of day, word-brose.

Named places have been dictionaried in
Ground's secret lexicon, its racial moan
Of etymology and cries of pain
That slit a summer wind and then were gone.

A mother calls her daughter from her door.
Her house, my stone illusion, hugs its hill.
From Eaglesham west to the rocky shore
Her cry is stretched across bog-asphodel.

The patronymic miles of grass and weddings,
Their festivals of gender, covenants,
Poor pre-industrially scattered steadings,
Ploughed-up davochs—old names, inhabitants.

And on my map is neither wall or fence,
But men and women and their revenue,
As, watching them, I utter into silence
A granary of whispers rinsed in dew.

LOCH MUSIC

I listen as recorded Bach
Restates the rhythms of a loch.
Through blends of dusk and dragonflies
A music settles on my eyes
Until I hear the living moors,
Sunk stones and shadowed conifers,
And what I hear is what I see,
A summer night's divinity.
And I am not administered
Tonight, but feel my life transferred
Beyond the realm of where I am
Into a personal extreme,
As on my wrist, my eager pulse
Counts out the blood of someone else.
Mist-moving trees proclaim a sense
Of sight without intelligence;
The intellects of water teach
A truth that's physical and rich.
I nourish nothing with the stars,
With minerals, as I disperse,
A scattering of quavered wash
As light against the wind as ash.

SHIPS

When a ship passes at night on the Clyde,
The swans in the reeds picking the oil from their feathers
Look up at the lights, the noise of new waves,
Against hill-climbing houses, malefic cranes.

A fine rain attaches itself to the ship like skin.
The lascars play poker, the Scottish mate looks
At the last lights, that one is Ayrshire,
Others on lonely rocks, or clubfooted peninsulas.

They leave restless boys without work in the river towns.
In their houses are faded pictures of fathers ringed
Among ships' complements in wartime, model destroyers,
Souvenirs from uncles deep in distant engine rooms.

Then the boys go out, down streets that look on water.
They say, 'I could have gone with them,'
A thousand times to themselves in the glass cafés,
Over their American soft drinks, into their empty hands.

ALAN BOLD

FENCES

Even in nature man makes divisions,
Mapping out territorial acquisitions
With stones that fence out fields and grass
As solid warnings against trespass.
Yet sheep in winter wear frozen cones of wool
That tinkle like pieces of steel.
And the animals refuse to be fenced in.
These stupid sheep blunder, baa out their din
And stupidly stray from their territory.
        This, of course, is allegory
In reverse. The sheep are sick
Of imitating man who likes to stick

To the bit he was born to,
Never wonderingly wandering in blue
Grass or green skies but instead
Fencing fields inside his head—
(Never seeing grass running like a green sea,
Rivers drifting into eternity,
Buttercups shaking their yellow heads,
Thistles blasting out of earthbound beds,
The erratic arrow of a swift
Winging its way through a wind drift)
—Fencing fields inside his head
And staying there.

The sheep flounder in the air.

STONY VISION

On the hillside where they come to cut trees
To keep warm through overcast winter days
He saw a stone on a treeless stretch of grass.

And it looked like a book dropped from heaven,
A monumental tome with all the answers,
A heavenly logos come to this hilly haven.

He held back, thinking if he came too close
It would be nothing but a stone, not
Commandments come to bring the world repose.

He held back and noticed that the others
Ignored it, walked past in their search for wood,
Being there solely as wood-gatherers.

He looked again: was it a stone
In the shape of a book, or a great message
Sent directly down for him alone?

Commonsense told him the object was a stone,
Nothing but a stone, so like the others
He passed by. Next morning it was gone.

RODERICK WATSON

GRANITE CITY ECLOGUE

Shines like frost   quartz hard   is worked with difficulty.

Predurable.   A source of pride in character and action
is in that glittering obduracy of mind   formidable
as Annie Davidson   —a relative 16 years dead
and not far removed   who left service
as a lady's maid   by plaiting her employer's braids
into the back of the bedroom chair   and slapped her face
carefully   had six children (and five survived).
Her life's pride   was always to have managed.

But if endurance is a virtue   it makes us accomplice
to suffering   and its verity a convenient motto
for the merchant fathers   who made more hose
out of less wool   by observing   what the girls wasted
at the end of the factory day   and stopping it.
For the men of standing   who built grace into Grecian banks
and baronial hotels   and for the owners in their time
the elders of the steam trawler   in quiet houses
with sweet gardens   risen   from the fish
the stink of the catch   silver   on rusted plating

dredged out of the North Sea   cold   blooded   teeming
the coin of that round and ruptured eye   bright as mica
exploding in the pan   brought in by the ton
on deck with frozen hands   split raw salt flesh
weeks out for days in town   drinking   spending
sick as a cat in the lavvie   and out for more
two suits on the door   Sunday shoes under the bed.
For fish does not last   at all   and ripeness counts
and people have to manage   and damned if they don't.

Little virtue then   in such prideful exercise of grip
and scorn for what doesn't hold   and little ease
in the hard word.   Nevertheless   I value true things
by their difficulty   —a resistance to the will—
and celebrate this desperate intransigence   in all creation:
for   at the last   I cannot credit grace
among accomplishments   in place of what is *here* and
    endures
nor deny the stern fathers   the merchant men
their inheritance   without accepting too
that ecstasy of opposition   which is how the son begins.

Defined by indirection   I am here
in the blossom of Cambridge   and away from home
    mostly.

TOM LEONARD

THE GOOD THIEF

heh jimmy
yawright ih
stull wayiz urryi
ih

heh jimmy
ma right insane yirra pape
ma right insane yirwanny us jimmy
see it nyir eyes
wanny uz

heh

hch jimmy
lookslik wirgonny miss thi gemm
gonny miss thi GEMM jimmy
nearly three a cloke thinoo

dork init
good jobe theyve gote thi lights

FEED MA LAMZ

Amyir gaffirz Gaffir. Hark.

　　nay fornirz ur communists
　　nay langwij
　　nay lip
　　nay laffn ina sunday
　　nay g.b.h. (septina wawr)
　　nay nooky huntn
　　nay tea-leaven
　　nay chanty rasslin
　　nay nooky huntn nix doar
　　nur kuvitn their ox

Oaky doaky. Stick way it
—rahl burn thi lohta yiz.

THE VOYEUR

what's your favourite word dearie
is it wee
I hope it's wee
wee's such a nice wee word
like a wee hairy dog
with two wee eyes
such a nice wee word to play with dearie
you can say it quickly
with a wee smile
and a wee glance to the side
or you can say it slowly dearie
with your mouth a wee bit open
and a wee sigh dearie
a wee sigh
put your wee head on my shoulder dearie
oh my
a great wee word
and Scottish
it makes you proud

STANLEY ROGER GREEN

TO A PEEVISH WOMAN

You occupied the royal suite of my soul
And complained of draughts
You held the keys to all the doors
And let them rust
You had a ringside seat at all my contests
And kept throwing in towels

You watched the dramas from the wings
I couldn't hear the prompter for your catcalls
The tears that arose to obscure the scene
Werc too salty, they would spoil your make-up
You viewed my universe from a planetarium
And thought the constellations ungainly

Together we rehearsed the music of the spheres
But you required a descant from others
The ripening diapason which engulfs
The sunset splendour which unites
Filled you with fear of harmony and the dark
You switched on artificial noons

Lady, you would ascend the staircase of heaven
And discover cobwebs at every baluster
You would find the robes and coiffures of the seraphim
Hopelessly out of fashion
And you would look around Creation and declare
That God had delusions of grandeur

THE OLD BING

A century ago deep dripping galleries were gutted
To build this monument above the wooded carse;
Now the bing is overwhelmed by dog-rose and bramble,
Veins of wild strawberry throb under bracken.

In winter keen hill winds and valley rains
Strip it bare revealing a gaunt memorial;
Stark in its grandeur the bing rears from the carse
Like the tumulus of a long-dead jarl or thane.

At its base a slow river ambles reflecting tall
Hills and still herons heraldic in twilight;
Not even the sighs of evening winds can recall
The anguished grunts of those nameless toilers

Who hacked a sparse living from grudging seams,
Cursed at roof-falls, mourned lost comrades,
Indifferent as moles to the cenotaph above them
Each day darkly rising, shouldering the sun.

CHRISTOPHER RUSH

STONE

Stone,
you occupy space so precisely
and with such joylessness and calm.
Envying your unequivocal existence,
such thereness, such fixity,
I pick you out of the sea's shifting reach
with graceless hands.

Stone,
you occupy time so spaciously
and with such preposterous aplomb.
I admire your immortal belonging. But whence
do you inhabit? Then or Now?
Not knowing, I place you back on the beach
with fleeting fingers.

MONDAY MORNING

The usual dreich set-tae—wund and wrack.
As I trauchle intae schule afore the bairnies
the cloods mell thegither i the lift.
I hunker doun at my desk, souch, an glower

at the windaes. First ava comes a spit o rain
like wee sherp preens, proggin. I haud ticht
the weekend's warmth. Watterdraps that wore awa
the stanes o Troy fund sma resistance

in me. They hing there on the gless
neutral as gravity, syne faa, wi the soonlessness
o empires. 'Pitter-patter owre the watter . . .'
Sune the rain's fair slivverin doun the panes,

the blurry gless pentin the mornin
wi that protective lee that windaes tell,
like art's cantraips, filmin the traith. Nou
the onding turns the faan leaves ootby

tae a broun smush. Nou the October wund
swurls roon the trees, an the lave o the saison
faas in flisters tae weet gress-graves.
The bell's jowin dirls on my jaw. Dourly

I yoke tae the week's affset, sweir tae tak
the dreel I've plooed wi roosty coulter owre an owre.
The bairns arrive. I grip the stilts, chalk an biro:
Whit trasherie will I turn up the day?

dreich, dreary, tedious; *wrack,* flying clouds; *trauchle,* trail; *mell thegither,* mix
together; *lift,* sky; *hunker,* squat; *souch,* sigh; *glower,* scowl; *ava,* of all; *preens,* pins;
proggin, pricking; *slivverin,* dribbling like saliva; *cantraips,* magical spells; *traith,*
truth; *onding,* heavy fall of rain; *ootby,* outside; *lave,* remainder; *flisters,* showers;
jowin, tolling; *dirls,* vibrates; *yoke,* begin; *affset,* pretence; *sweir,* reluctant; *dreel,*
furrow; *trasherie,* rubbish

VALERIE GILLIES

DEERHOUNDS

Admit the lives more valuable
than our life, than the bodies we bear
more beautiful: tall grey dogs,

what huntsman, what dogboy loosed you
on our slow hearts
and let you slaughter them?

Long dogs, you move with air
belling the vault of your ribcage.
You subdue the miles below your hocks.

Levelled out in speed across wayless country,
over the open grassmoor that is paradise,
the onset of your going undulates the ground.

The bracken hurdles below your height,
the rushes make way for you;
your hard eyes hold in sight the rapid hills.

Brace of deerhounds, a matched two!
Intent, all flame, is what quickens
those long throats thonged with leather.

YOUNG HARPER

Above Tweed Green levels
Maeve first raises the harp.

Prosper her hand that plucks
then clenches fist like a jockey.

Grip inside thighs
the colt with a cropped mane.

Turn blades on the curved neck
bristling with spigots.

Out from the rosewood forest
came this foal of strung nerve.

Stand in your grainy coat,
let her lift elbows over you.

Keep her thumbs bent
and fingers hard to do the playing:

Eight summers made them, clarsach,
I freely give you my elder daughter.

LIZ LOCHHEAD

NOISES IN THE DARK

(Anatolia, April 74)

The four a.m. call to the faithful wakes us,
its three-time off-key harmony of drones and wails.
Above our heads I snap the lightcord but the power fails
as usual leaving us in the dark. Tomorrow takes us
who knows where. What ruins? What towns? What smells?
Nothing shakes us.
Where we touch today's too painful sunburn sticks and sears
apart again. Faithful to something three long years
no fear, no final foreign dark quite breaks us.

Hotel habitues,
those ritually faithful wash their feet. Old plumbing grumbles.
The tap-leak in our rust-ringed basin tickles
irritant, incessant, an itch out of the dark. Whitewash
    crumbles
from the wall where the brittle cockroach trickles.
Fretful, faithful, wide to the dark, can we ever forget
this shabby town hotel, the shadow of the minaret?
Was that human or bird or animal? What cried?
The dark smear across our wall still unidentified.

POPPIES

My father said she'd be fined
at best, jailed maybe, the lady
whose high heels shattered the silence.
I sat on his knee, we were listening
to the silence on the radio.
My mother tutted, oh that it was terrible,
as over our air
those sharp heeltaps struck steel, rang clear
as a burst of gunfire or a laugh
through those wired-up silent streets around the Cenotaph.
Respect.
Remembrance.
Surely when all was said
three minutes silence in November
wasn't much to ask for, for the dead?
Poppies on the mantelpiece, the photograph
of a boy in a forage cap, the polished
walnut veneer of the wireless,
the buzzing in the ears and when
the silence ended the heldfire voice

of the commentator, who was shocked,
naturally, but not
wanting to make too much of it.
Why did she do it?
Was she taken sick—but that was no
excuse, on the radio it said,
couldn't you picture it?
how grown soldiers buttoned in their uniforms
keeled over, fell like flies
trying to keep up the silence.
Maybe it was looking at the khaki button eye
and the woundwire stem
of the redrag poppy
pinned in her proper lapel
that made the lady stick a bloody bunch of them
behind her ear
and clash those high heels across the square,
a dancer.

POEM FOR MY SISTER

My little sister likes to try my shoes,
to strut in them,
admire her spindle-thin twelve-year-old legs
in this season's styles.
She says they fit her perfectly,
but wobbles
on their high heels, they're
hard to balance.

I like to watch my little sister
playing hopscotch,
admire the neat hops-and-skips of her,
their quick peck,
never-missing their mark, not
over-stepping the line.
She is competent at peever.

I try to warn my little sister
about unsuitable shoes,
point out my own distorted feet, the callouses,
odd patches of hard skin.
I should not like to see her
in *my* shoes.
I wish she could stay
sure footed,
         sensibly shod.

RAYMOND VETTESE

HUE O VIRR

Nae end tae the life o the green earth!
The teuchest crust o winter canna haud it.
In the derkness o the season the gowden seed
curl ticht for the lowp—ae whack o sun
cracks them oot and up they shog,
relentless, like the teethin o bairns,
rivin, rivin, till eence mair the world's
crooned, wi emeraud—the hue o virr,
the ageless, aye-bidan colour o smeddum.

virr, vigour; *teuchest,* toughest; *lowp,* leap; *ae,* one single; *whack,* cut; *shog,* jolt; *rivin,* bursting asunder; *eence,* once; *emeraud,* emerald; *aye-bidan,* eternal; *smeddum,* mettle

REEL O LOVE

The lang stracht ahent:
a life weel-mappit,
nae howe nor brae—
aa plain sailin.

Syne you cam an sent it reelin!

Afore me nou
this corkscrew path
an me
dizzy wi the turns o't
yet wild aa the same wi sic a joy
I wadna care gin I never kent again
grund aneath me!

stracht, straight; *howe*, valley; *brae*, hill

ANDREW GREIG

IN THE TOOL-SHED

'Hummingbirds' he said, and spat. Winged tongues
hovered in the half-light of their names;
cat, cobra, cockatoo rose hissing from the juice.
Piece-time in Africa, amid the terrapins
and jerrycans! Steam swirled above the Congo
of his cup, mangrove-rooted fingers plugged the air—

'Baboons? Make sure you look them in the eyes.' Birds
of paradise! Parrots, paraffin, parakeets
flashed blue and raucous through
thickets of swoe, scythe, riddle, adze.
He sat bow-backed and slack in the dark
heart of his kingdom—creator, guide
in that jungle of sounds, boxes, cloches, canes,
twine, twill, galoshes, jumbled all
across, over, through and into one another
from floor to roof, prowled by fabled carnivores,
the jaguar! the secataurs! Words poke
wet muzzles through reeds of sound
grown enormous overnight. Twin depths
of pitch and pitcher! Elephants lean
patiently upon their ponderous names.
They come in clutches: azaleas, zebras, zambesi.
Orchids, oranges, oran-utangs hang
from their common mouth. Lemming, gorilla, lynx
slink nose to tail through mango groves,
drenched in this sibilant monsoon: moonstone, machettes,
peacocks, paw-paws, lepers, leopards—the walls
are creaking but hold them all, swaying, sweating,
in that dark continent between the ears.
Easy, easy genesis! Old witchdoctor, gardener,
deity of the shed, I grew that garden
from his words, caught the fever
pitch of his Niagara; I follow still
the Orinoco of his blue forearm veins
that beat among the talking drums
of all my childhood afternoons.

IN GALLOWAY

In Galloway the drystane dykes that curl
like smoke over the shoulder of the hill
are built with holes
through which sky shows and spindrift birls,
so the wind is baffled but not barred
lest drifting snow smoors a sheltering herd.

There is an art in framing holes
and in the space between the stones.
Structures pared to the bone—
the line that pleases by what's not there
or drydykes laced across the whirling air.

ROBERT CRAWFORD

THE SCOTTISH NATIONAL CUSHION SURVEY

Our heritage of Scottish cushions is dying.
Teams of careful young people in training schemes
Arrived through a government incentive, counting
Every cushion. In Saltcoats, through frosty Lanark.
They even searched round Callanish
For any they'd missed. There are no more Scottish cushions
Lamented the papers. Photographs appeared
Of the last cushion found in Gaeldom.
Silk cushions, pin cushions, pulpit cushions.
We must preserve our inheritance.

So the museums were built: The Palace of Cushions, the
    National
Museum of Soft Seating, and life went on elsewhere
Outside Scotland. The final Addendum was published
Of *Omnes Pulvini Caledonii.*
Drama documentaries. A chapter closed.
And silently in Glasgow quick hands began
Angrily making cushions.